"*MINIMUM REQUIRED EQUIPMENT*" chart on Page 186
reprinted with permission of
Department of Navigation and
Ocean Development,
State of California

Cover photo courtesy of
BIG BEAR LAKE VALLEY
CHAMBER OF COMMERCE

First Printing, September 1975
Second Printing (revised), April 1976
Third Printing (revised), February 1978
Fourth Printing (revised), August 1979
Fifth Printing (revised), March 1981
Sixth Printing (revised), September 1982
Seventh Printing (revised), January 1985
Eighth Printing (revised), February 1987
Ninth Printing (revised), February 1989
Tenth Printing (revised), February 1991
Eleventh Printing (revised), April 1993
Twelfth Printing (revised), January 1995
Thirteenth Printing (revised), September 1996

INDEX BY LAKES

LAKE RECREATION
IN
SOUTHERN CALIFORNIA

FROM

MONTEREY COUNTY
(Lake San Antonio)

TO

MEXICO

BY

HERSCHELL WHITMER
AND
SCOTT WHITMER

Library of Congress Catalog Card #87-50128
Library of Congress #ISSN 0892-2381
ISBN #09619015-4-3

Published by HERSCHELL WHITMER ASSOCIATES

Herschell with Casitas 10.2 pound.

Scott with 11.5 Castiac lunker.

INDEX BY LAKES (continued)

INDEX BY LAKES (continued)

FISHING INFORMATION

For San Diego City Lakes, call (619) 465-FISH. You will get up-to-date information on the following lakes:

EL CAPITAN
HODGES
MIRAMAR
MURRAY
OTAY, LOWER
OTAY, UPPER
SAN VICENTE
SUTHERLAND
BARRETT

REPORT VIOLATIONS AND POACHING
CAL-TIP   1-(800)-952-5400
8:00 a.m. - 5:00 p.m. Monday through Friday

CONSERVE OUR RESOURCES!

NOTE: You may fish with two poles at the same time in lakes and reservoirs where the Department of Fish and Game regulations apply. The second pole permit is $8.15 in addition to the basic license fee.

INDEX BY COUNTIES

INDEX BY COUNTIES (continued)

INDEX BY COUNTIES (continued)

SAN DIEGO COUNTY

SAN LUIS OBISPO COUNTY

INDEX BY COUNTIES (continued)

o o o o

STATE OF CALIFORNIA
DEPARTMENTS OF FISH AND GAME

STATE OFFICE   (916) 653-7664
1416 NINTH STREET, SACRAMENTO, CA 94244

REGION #3   (707) 944-5500
7329 SILVERWOOD TRAIL, YOUNTVILLE, CA 94558

REGION #4   (209) 222-3761
1234 EAST SHAW AVENUE, FRESNO, CA 93710

REGION #5   (310) 590-5132
330 GOLDEN SHORE, LONG BEACH, CA 90802

4949 VIEW RIDGE AVENUE, SAN DIEGO, CA 92123   (619) 467-4201
(New office in San Diego)

FOREWORD

This book was written for the person who enjoys fresh water lakes, be he fisherman, boater, camper, or nature lover. The person who wants to know where to go, how to get there, and what to expect in the way of costs, limits, bait, and other facilities that are available.

By using the information in this book, anyone can plan sensibly for his trip, eliminate the unnecessary, and in most cases can verify the information by phone if desired.

The writer has tried to include all lakes in the selected area and to cover each lake as completely as possible with information that would be useful to fishermen and campers.

To be truthful, I have always wanted a book like this and it wasn't available . . . so I wrote it.

I hope you find it as enjoyable in the using as Scott and I have in the writing and revising.

Good fishing and camping.

Sincerely,

Herschell Whitmer

NOTE TO THE USER:

All information contained herein was as accurate as could be obtained at the time of writing.

Since all prices, policies, and regulations are subject to change due to various reasons, verifications can be made by phone.

All maps are not scale and are to show relative positions only. Mileages are approximate and may vary somewhat with different routes taken to the lakes.

Each lake's rules and regulations governing the use of inflatable boats, and the minimum boat equipment requirements of the State of California have been added on Pages 182 through 185.

Also, some of the lakes that are listed as closed to the public may be opened at a later date. Future changes will be noted in subsequent editions.

ACKNOWLEDGEMENT

We would like to express our gratitude to those who were so cooperative in furnishing the information contained in this book:

All the lake managers, concessionaires, U.S. Forest Service and staff, newspaper editors, Departments of Parks and Recreation of the eleven counties, City Park and Recreation Departments, Irrigation and Water District Managers, the State Department of Water Resources, State Department of Parks and Recreation, Chambers of Commerce, U.S. Army Corps of Engineers, the Department of Fish & Game, Los Angeles County Flood Control District – and anyone we might have missed.

To our secretary who has typed and re-typed enough pages preparing this book to fill 50 books.

Dedicated: To my wife, Shirley.

Maps by William H. Whitmer

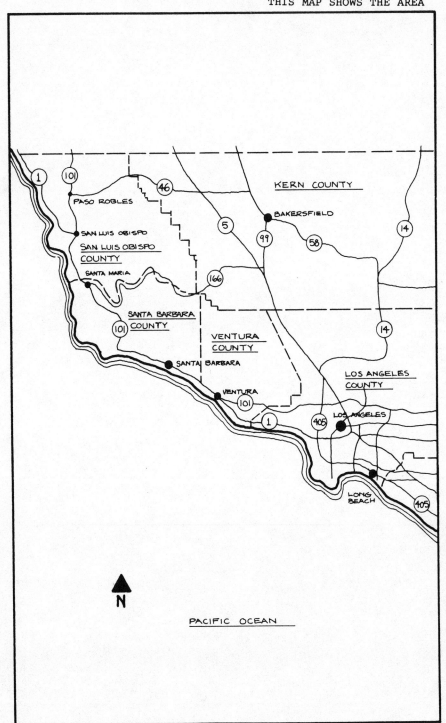

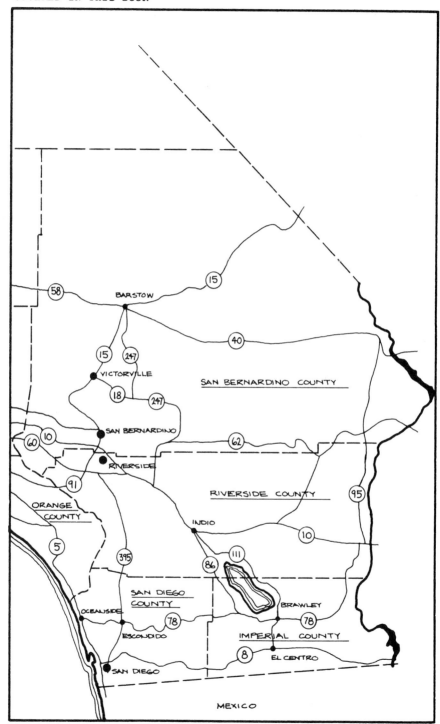

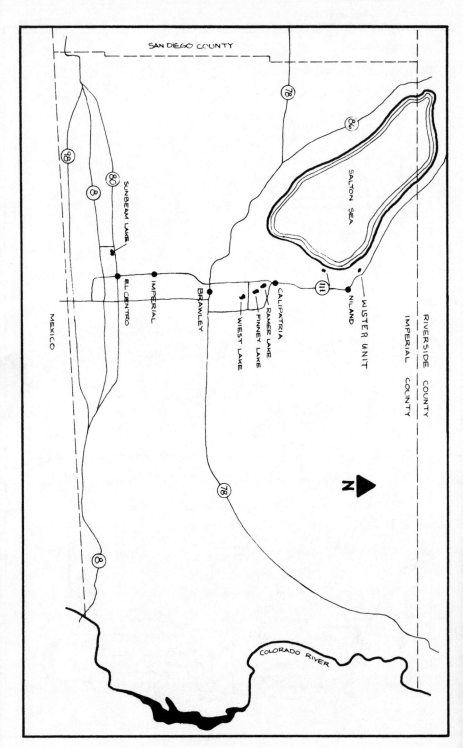

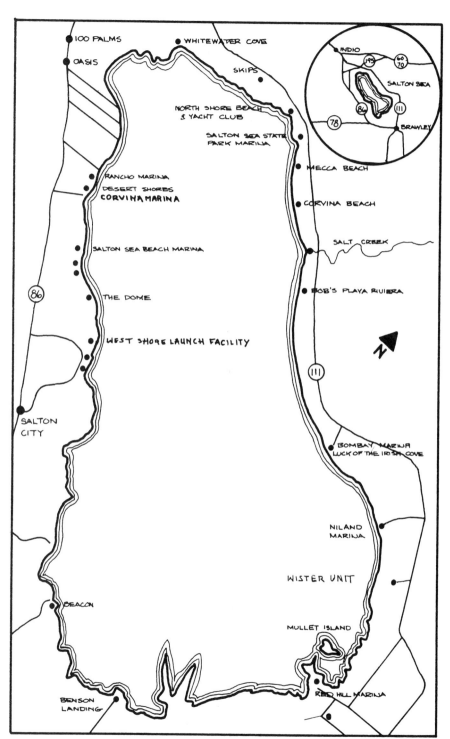

100 PALMS
OASIS
WHITEWATER COVE
SKIPS
NORTH SHORE BEACH & YACHT CLUB
SALTON SEA STATE PARK MARINA
RANCHO MARINA
DESERT SHORES
CORVINA MARINA
SALTON SEA BEACH MARINA
THE DOME
WEST SHORE LAUNCH FACILITY
SALTON CITY
BEACON
BENSON LANDING

INDIO
SALTON SEA
BRAWLEY

MECCA BEACH
CORVINA BEACH
SALT CREEK
BOB'S PLAYA RIVIERA
BOMBAY MARINA
LUCK OF THE IRISH COVE
NILAND MARINA
WISTER UNIT
MULLET ISLAND
RED HILL MARINA

SALTON SEA

Imperial and Riverside Counties

Elevation, 234' below sea level   Surface 360 sq. miles

Salton Sea is approximately 140 miles southeast of Los Angeles. Take Hwy 10 or 60 east to Indio then three miles to Coachella. Here you take Hwy 111 (left) to get to all north shore camps and marinas OR take Hwy 86 (right) to get to all the south shore marinas and camps.

NOTE TO READERS
Since 1975 the water level has continually risen and covered many camping and docking facilities at various marinas. Now, the water is receding. It would be wise to confirm the availability of the facilities by phone before making your trip.

OPEN   Year round. You may fish 24 hours a day.

FEES   State fishing license required. No fee for fishing in the lake. There is a charge (auto) to use the State Park North Side facilities: $5.00 per day or $75.00 per year auto permit. Age 62: $1.00 discount. Dog permit: $1.00 per day. Guide dog free — Disabled 1/2 price.

BOAT RENTALS   There are no boat rentals at this time (1996).

BOAT LAUNCH   There are many boat launching ramps starting with State Park — North Shore, $5.00 per launch or $50.00 for annual launching permit, includes annual day use. Ask for summer discounts.

FREE LAUNCH — Imperial County Parks: (619) 339-4384

Niland Marina   CLOSED TEMPORARILY
Red Hill Marina (no gas)   (619) 348-2310

PRIVATE MARINA LAUNCHING from $5.00 to $9.00 launching charge.

NORTH AND EAST SHORE

North Shore Marina	(619) 393-3891
Salton Sea State Park Marina	(619) 393-3052
Bombay Marina	

SOUTH AND WEST SHORE

Desert Shores Trailer Park	(619) 395-5280
Desert Shores Marina	(619) 395-5280
Salton Sea Beach Marina	(619) 395-5212
Westshores RV Park & Marina	(619) 394-4755
Benson Landing (flooded)	(No Phone)

FISH & LIMIT	Corvina - 5; Croaker, Tilipia and Sargo - No limit.
FISH CLEANING	There are excellent cleaning facilities at the State Park Marina, north side. Some of the other marinas have facilities as well.
BAIT	Almost any kind of live bait, minnows, mudsuckers, and cut bait OK. See Article 3, Section 4.15, D.F.G. Regs.
SWIMMING	There are swimming beaches all around the sea. Many places have showers for swimmers as well. Waders and tube fishing OK.
PICNICKING	Yes. State Park has facilities; Imperial County Parks have picnic areas; many of the marinas have facilities.
WATERSKI	Yes. Large area. Jetski OK.
SAILING WINDSURF	Yes - Excellent. BUT, PLEASE SEE "CAUTION" NEXT PAGE.
CAMPING	Salton Sea State Park (619) 393-3052. Reservations may be made through DESTINET 1-800-444-7275. Headquarters Area and Mecca Beach have water, good restrooms, and showers. Rates for September 1 through May 31 - day use $5.00; camping $13.00 weeknights, $14.00 Friday and Saturday; $15.00 full hook-ups, $19.00 weeknights, $20.00 Friday and Saturday. Additional vehicle $5.00 extra. Rates for June 1 through August 31 - day use $4.00; camping $10.00 per night, $15.00 full hook-ups, $14.00 per night. Seniors get $2.00 camping discount year round. Disabled 1/2 price.

Corvina, Salt Creek, and Bombay Beach Campground are primitive campgrounds. Salt Creek has no water. September 1 through May 31 - day use $5.00, camping $7.00 per night. June 1 through August 31 - day use $4.00, camping $6.00 per night. Age 62 has discount.

Niland Marina - Closed temporarily.

Red Hill Marina (619) 348-2310: Boat launch and day use, $3.00 charge; camping, $7.00 per night; $5.00 extra for electricity and water; restrooms and the showers free for campers.

Most all marinas listed under Boat Launch Section have camping. Some with full hook-ups from $19.00 to $25.00 per night. Call for exact facilities and charges.

STORES	Most marinas have stores where you can buy bait, food, drink, fishing gear, gas, oil, ice, and all types of supplies.
MOTELS	There are numerous motels from Indio along Hwy 86 and at the various settlements on the south shore.
HUNTING	Yes. Waterfowl and upland game. Call (310) 590-5132 for full information as to areas and seasons.
DUNE BUGGIES MOTOR-BIKES	There are numerous places to ride, but it is wise to check with local authorities and businessmen to make sure of each area.
GENERAL	Prior to 1905 Salton Sea was a gleaming white salt flat that was left after a large sea of water had evaporated over hundreds of years. In that year, an irrigation diversion dam was broken by the Colorado River flood waters near Yuma and ran for two years, forming a lake of 20x45 miles. Since that time, the evaporation brought the lake down to its present size and it remains fairly constant due to the run-off from the various irrigation drainage ditches that drain into it.

The water is slightly saltier than the ocean and will support fish that are native to ocean waters. In the early '50s the California Department of Fish and Game made plants of orange mouth corvina, sargo and gulf croaker. All three have flourished and have made Salton Sea an excellent fishing lake. Corvina usually run from 10 to 15 pounds, but some to 36 pounds have been caught. Sargo, tilipia and croaker can be caught readily from 1 to 2 pounds on shrimp, cut bait, or worms.

The best fishing occurs during the late spring to early fall when temperatures are 90° and above.

CAUTION Boaters should be cautious of sudden winds that occur at times, as they produce large waves very quickly and it becomes unsafe, especially for the smaller boats. It is always advisable to check the weather forecasts and adhere to the boating regulations.

The Salton Sea area has additional activities, such as rock-hunting, hiking, and all those found at other desert recreational communities. A trip to Salton Sea provides an unusual experience for the whole family.

IMPERIAL COUNTY

CANALS

There are approximately 3,000 miles of canals running through Imperial Valley. All of them have Bass, 10 limit (no size limit), large channel catfish, 10 limit; striper bass, 10 limit (no size limit); crappie, 25 limit; bluegill, no limit.

Two species of tilipia were introduced some years back to control the vegetation in the canals. These fish have since multiplied and are now quite numerous throughout the canal network. These fish grow to three or four pounds, but the majority of the ones caught are pan size. Tilipia resemble a sunfish and are quite good to eat. There is no limit to the number you catch.

Fishermen camp along these canals in their self-contained campers, trailers, and RVs to catch these large catfish. Be careful with children as these banks are steep and almost impossible to climb.

No boats are allowed, and no swimming.

For hunters and fishermen who want more information as to catches and places to hunt and fish, call the Yellow Mart Stores (619) 347-1107, or write to the store at 82850 Miles Avenue, Indio, CA 92201. You can get all fishing, hunting, and camping supplies here as well as information on the canals and Salton Sea.

NOTE: The All American Canal from the Central Main Turnout west, and waters west of the Salton Sea are now open (1996) to all fishing and bait collecting.

o o o o

FINNEY-RAMER LAKES UNIT

Highway 111, Calipatria, CA 92233
Phone: Ranger (619) 359-0577

Elevation, 90' below sea level   Surface Acres 1,000

Finney-Ramer Lakes are located approximately 185 miles southeast of Los Angeles. Take Hwy 10 to Indio. Go south from Indio on Hwy 111 for 64 miles (2 miles through Calipatria) past Dowden Road. Turn east on next road, 1 mile to Lower Ramer Lake.

This lake complex is made up of four lakes: Upper and Lower Finney; and, Upper and Lower Ramer.

The Finney-Ramer Unit is open year round. State Fish & Game Rules apply.

State license required. There are no use fees; use permits are self-registered each day.

There are no boat rentals; however, there is a launch for row boats, paddle boats, and canoes only. There are only electric motors allowed. No charge for launching boats.

Fish and Limit: Bass – 10 (no size limit); cats – 10; crappie – 25; bluegill – no limit. There are no fish cleaning facilities.

Waterdogs, mudsuckers, and worms OK. See Section 4.15 of the California Sports Fishing Regulations for allowable minnows.

No swimming.

Finney-Ramer is not really set up for picnicking; and with electric motors allowed, there is no water skiing. Only very small sailboats can be accommodated.

There are approximately 30 campsites. Trailers, campers, and tents OK. Very rustic. No fee – first come, first served; rustic restrooms; no water; no electricity. Seven-day limit, 14 days per year.

There are stores and motels nearby in Brawley and Calipatria.

There is hunting in season for waterfowl, rabbits, quail, and dove. (619) 359-0577 for information.

The Finney-Ramer Unit is under the jurisdiction of the Resources Agency Department of Fish and Game. Local Ranger is on Hwy 111, Calipatria, CA 92233 – (619) 359-0577.

The area is well-known for its waterfowl hunting, but it is also a good fishing complex. Most people fish from the bank as there are no boat rentals and only row boats can be launched.

Needless to say, this area gets hot in the summer; so go prepared.

NOTE: There are three additional ponds, Sheldon Pond, Guillen Pond, and Culver Pond, adjacent to Upper and Lower Finney that are fishable as well. Finney-Ramey rules apply.

o o o o

SUNBEAM LAKE

Park Ranger – (619) 352-3308

Elevation – below sea level   Surface Acres Approx. 12

Sunbeam Lake is located approximately 207 miles southeast of Los Angeles in the Southwest corner of Imperial County. From Los Angeles take Hwy 10 to Indio; from Indio take Hwy 86 through Brawley and Imperial to Hwy 8. Turn west on Hwy 8 approximately six miles to Drew Road; north on Drew Road for half a mile to the lake.

From San Diego, come east on Hwy 8 to Drew Road, turn north half a mile.

Sunbeam is really two small lakes; both are approximately 100' wide and half mile long. They are open year round to fishing and camping. No fishing fee, just state fishing license required.

The lakes have trout - 5 (planted in cool weather); bass - 10 (no size limit); catfish - 10 limit; crappie - 25; bluegill, no limit. No fish cleaning facilities. Waterdogs, mudsuckers, and worms OK. See Section 4.15 of the California Sports Fishing Regulations for allowable minnows.

No boat rentals. Boat launch and day use of park, $2.00. Inflatables - no size limit - must be seaworthy and one life jacket per passenger.

During Spring, Summer, and Fall there is swimming, with a lifeguard provided.

Camping - Sunbeam Lake RV Camp is new with 309 full hook-up sites. $18.00 per night; $105.00 per week; $300.00 per month. Price includes cable TV with use of Clubhouse, restrooms, hot showers, laundromat, shuffle board, and more. For reservations call (619) 352-7154.

Skiing and jetskis OK.

For information call Ranger (619) 352-3308 or write Sunbeam Lake, 155 South 11th Street, Suite "C", El Centro, CA 92243.

o o o o

WEIST LAKE

Rutherford Road, Brawley, CA 92227
(Between Hwys 111 and 115)
Phone: (619) 344-3712

Elevation, 85 feet below sea level   Surface Acres Approx. 55

Weist Lake is located approximately 187 miles southeast of Los Angeles. Take Hwy 10 from Los Angeles to Indio; go through Indio on Hwy 111 approximately 65 miles to Rutherford Road (3 miles past Calipatria), turn east 2 miles to lake.

Lake Weist is open year round. No fee. Fishermen must have state license.

The lake has trout - 5 (planted in cool weather); catfish - 10 limit; bass - 10 (no size limit); crappie - 25; bluegill, no limit. No fish cleaning facilities.

Waterdogs, mudsuckers, and worms OK. See Section 4.15 of the California Sports Fishing Regulations for allowable minnows.

During Spring, Summer, and Fall there is swimming, with a life guard provided.

Day use of park, $2.00 per vehicle; boat launch free; there are no boat rentals. Inflatables - no size limit - must be seaworthy and one approved lifejacket per passenger.

There are 30 or more campsites with water for $7.00 per night; $5.00 extra for electricity; hot showers free. Dump station for RVs.

There is water skiing; picnicking with tables, shade ramadas, and barbeque pits.

There is no concession so bring anything you might need.

Weist Lake is under the jurisdiction of Imperial county Department of Parks & Recreations, 1002 State Street, El Centro, CA 92243. For information, call Ranger at (619) 344-3712.

o o o o

WISTER UNIT
OF THE IMPERIAL WILDLIFE AREA

Route 1, Box 6, Niland, Ca 92257
Phone: (619) 359-0577

Elevation – 200' below sea level   Surface acres 400

Wister Unit is located approximately 175 miles southeast of Los Angeles. Take Hwy 10 to Indio; take Hwy 111 south 57 miles to Davis Road (4½ miles north of Niland); turn right ¼ mile to office for permit to enter the area.

Wister Unit is open 24 hours per day, 365 days per year. From mid-October through mid-January only a portion (seven ponds of 200 acres) is open to fishermen. The balance is open only to waterfowl hunters.

There are no parking or fishing fees for those who have a fishing, hunting, or trapper's license. Others pay $2.50. You must obtain a permit when you enter. State fishing licenses required.

There are no boat rentals. Hand portable boats and electric motors are allowed.

There are bass, 10 (no size limit); cats, 10; crappie, 25; bluegill and bullhead, no limit. Waterdogs, mud suckers, crawfish, and worms OK. See California Sports Fishing Regulations, Section 4.15 for allowable minnows. There are no fish cleaning facilities and there is no swimming.

There are approximately 30 primitive sites for campers. You may stay up to 7 days – 14 days per year. There is no charge.

No stores at Wister; nearest would be 4½ miles in Niland.

Hunting: Waterfowl, dove, pheasants, quail, and rabbits in season. Call for information (619) 359-0577.

The Wister area gets mighty hot during Summer months. Be sure to bring what you need in the way of bait, food, drinks, ice, and a couple of brews because its 4½ miles to the nearest store.

The Wister Unit is under the jurisdiction of the State Department of Fish and Game, Wildlife Management, HCO-1, Box 6, Niland, CA 92257; Phone (619) 359-0577.

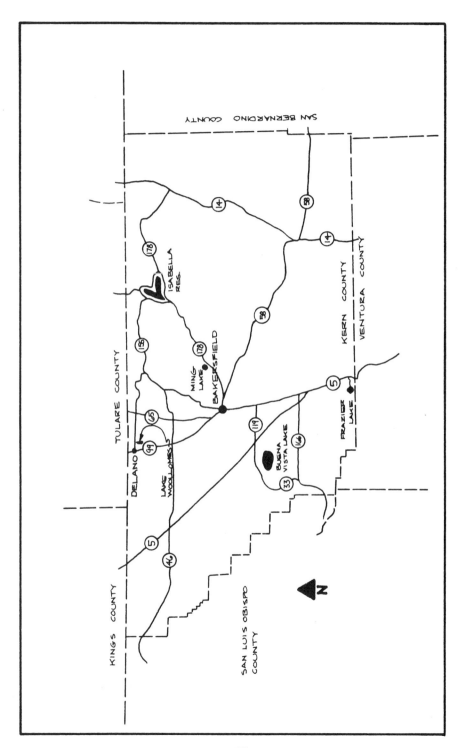

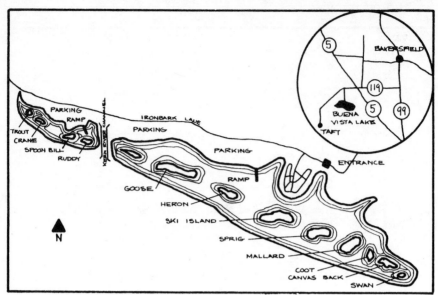

BUENA VISTA LAKE

P. O. Box 1042, Taft, CA 93268
Phones: Concession (805) 763-1770
Gate: (805) 861-2063   Elevation, 294 feet
LAKE WEBB   Surface Acres 873
LAKE EVANS   Surface Acres 86

The Buena Vista Lakes are located 115 miles northwest of Los Angeles and 23 miles southwest of Bakersfield. From Los Angeles take Hwy 5 north over the Ridge Route. Stay on Hwy 5 twenty miles past Wheeler Ridge to Hwy 119. Turn west on Hwy 119, go approximately 2 miles to Lake Road, turn left to lake.

OPEN & FEES

Year round, 6 a.m. to 10 p.m. for day use. State fishing license required. Auto: $5.00 per day up to 10 people; trout fishing – adult, $5.00; children (8 to 15 years), $1.00; $3.00 per day for dogs. Limit 2 dogs.

BOAT RENTAL

(805) 763-1770. The only rentals at this time (1996) are jetskis and waterskis.

BOAT LAUNCH

There are paved ramps: Two lanes in Lake Evans and four lanes in Lake Webb. Minimum size 7'6", powered by wind or sail. 11' applies to all power boats, canoes, and inflatables (Must have two compartments). State regulations apply.

Launch permit: $7.00 per day; $40.00 per year; good at all Kern County Lakes. Speed limit: 5 mph at Lake Evans (jetski area only); Lake Webb: 45 mph. Mooring available: $5.00 per day; $25 per week; $50 per month; $300 per year.

FISH & LIMITS	Bass (12" size limit) – 5; striped bass – 5; trout – 5; catfish, all kinds – 20; crappie – 25; bluegill, no limit. Two excellent fish cleaning facilities with modern disposers.
BAIT	Live bait OK, including waterdogs, mudsuckers, crawfish, minnows, worms, and lures.
SWIMMING	In lagoons only; waders OK in lagoon; no tube fishing.
PICNICKING	Yes. Excellent facilities (250 sites) with deep pit barbeques, including one group area for 400 people and two for at least 25 people each. These may be reserved for a fee.
WATERSKI JETSKI	Yes. Waterski in Lake Webb only – within markers. Jetski in both lakes in special marked areas.
HUNTING	No.

SAILING – WINDSURF – Yes. Check sailing areas. In both lakes.

MOTOR-BIKES	All motorbikes must be street legal and ridden on roads only. Daily fee required.
CAMPING	Yes. 132 units. $21 to $26 per day with utilities; $18 to $22 per day without utilities. Limited stay: 14 days in any 31-day period. Off season: Half price and 30-day maximum stay. Call DESTINET (800) 950-7275 for reservations.
STORES	Concession (805) 763-1770 has snack bar, gas-propane, licenses, groceries, ice, drinks, bait, fishing and camping supplies. Other stores are 17 miles away in Taft or 23 miles away in Bakersfield.
MOTELS	Closest motels are in Taft, 17 miles southwest OR Bakersfield, 23 miles northeast.
GENERAL	The Buena Vista Aquatic Recreation Area consists of 1,586 acres and is under the jurisdiction of the Kern County Parks and Recreation Department, 1110 Golden State Highway, Bakersfield, CA 93301; (805) 861-2345.

The Buena Vista Aquatic Recreation Area consists of 1,586 acres and is under the jurisdiction of the Kern County Parks and Recreation Department, 1110 Golden State Highway, Bakersfield, CA 93301; (805) 861-2345.

Both lakes were dry until April 1973. They have been stocked with bass, bluegill, crappie, trout, striped bass, white, blue, and channel cats. Bass up to 8 lbs. have been caught; crappie in the 3-pounder class; stripers to 32 pounds; cats over 50 lbs. (June 1993); and trout up to 9 lbs. 7 oz. have been caught.

This is an excellent area for the whole family to enjoy an outing. It is just over two hours from downtown Los Angeles.

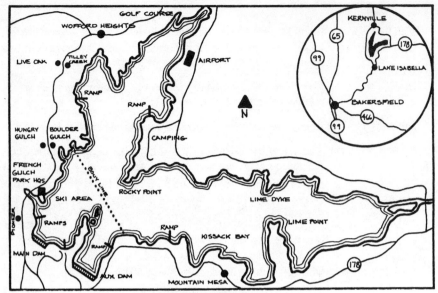

LAKE ISABELLA

Kern County California
Phone: (619) 379-5646

Kern River Valley Visitors Council	(619) 379-5646
Kernville Chamber of Commerce	(619) 376-2629

Elevation, 2,650 feet   Surface Acres, 11,200

Lake Isabella is located 163 miles north of Los Angeles. Take Hwy 5 north over the Ridge Route, down 4 miles past Wheeler Ridge; turn right on the Lake Isabella-Arvin turn-off. Follow to Hwy 178; turn right, go 41 miles up Kern River to the lake.

OPEN & FEES

Isabella is open 24 hours daily, year round. You can fish at night if you want, from the shore. Kern River above and below dam, open year round. State license required. No fishing permit required.

BOAT RENTALS

There are three marinas on Lake Isabella where boats can be rented: Ski boats, pontoon boats, pleasure boats, and Wave Runners available. (Rates vary somewhat at each marina.)
1. Dean's North Fork Marina   (619) 376-1812
2. French Gulch Marina   (619) 379-8774
3. Kern Valley Marina   (619) 379-1634

Fishing Boats:	Per Day	Half Day
With 8 HP	$40 and up	$30 and up
With 10 HP	$45 and up	$35 and up
With 15 HP	$50 and up	$40 and up

BOAT SLIP RENTALS	$10.00 per day; $45 per week; $100 per month 530 per year
BOAT LAUNCH	Boats 7' to 11' min; must be powered by wind or motor. This includes Jetskis and Windsurfers. These plus boats from 11' to 30' may use whole lake. All must have $20.00 lake use permit obtainable at all three marinas and at Crossroads Texaco station located at the corner of Isabella Blvd. and Hwy 155 – (619) 379-8170. Sail board permits are $15.00 per year. With permit you may launch free at six launch sites. There are four concrete ramps: one at Campsite #9 on the east side of north fork; one just east of the auxiliary dam on the south shore; one 1 mile from auxiliary dam on the south shore; and one between the main and auxiliary dam. There are two black top ramps. One on north shore, just past main dam on Pioneer Campsite; one on the west side of north fork next to Tilly Creek Camp.
INFLAT-ABLES & CANOES	Minimum 11' – must have state registration and must comply with state regulations.
FISH & LIMITS	Bass, 5 (12" size limit); blue catfish, 20; crappie, 25; bluegill and bullhead, no limit. Trout, 5. All campgrounds have fish cleaning facilities.
BAIT	No outside minnows, shad, or mudsuckers allowed. Waterdogs, crawfish, worms, crickets, and lures OK.
SWIMMING	Yes, within 200' of shore – Tilly Creek area. Waders and tube fishing OK, 100 yards from shore.
PICNICKING	Yes, many campgrounds, tables, etc.

WATERSKI – JETSKI – Yes, including windsurfing. May use whole lake.

MOTOR-CYCLES	Street legal – on roads only. Off-road vehicles check for usable areas.
SAILING	Yes, minimum 7'; maximum 30' in length. Use whole lake.
HUNTING	Quail, dove, chukkar deer, and bear in season. For information call (209) 222-3761, or write the Kern River Valley Visitors' Council, P. O. Box "O", Lake Isabella, CA 93240.
HORSEBACK RIDING	Yes. There are several stables and unlimited riding areas.
RIVER RAFTING	Yes. Kern River Tours (619) 379-4616; or, Chuck Richards Whitewater (619) 379-4444 or Outdoor Adventures 1-800-323-4234 or Sierra South Mountain Sports (619) 376-3745 and White Water Voyages 1-800-488-7238.

CAMPING   There are 8 campgrounds around the lake on a first come, first served basis. Five are improved, total 630 units. $14.00 per site from April 1 through September 30. Restrooms, water, and hot showers. There are six more campgrounds along the Kern River from Kernville on past Road's End. For group area reservations and rates, call 1 (800) 280-2267. For additional information call (619) 379-5646 or (619) 376-3781.

There is a KOA (Lake Isabella KOA) campground eleven miles east of the dam at 15627 Highway 178, Weldon, CA 93283, Phone: (619) 378-2001. This camp has 104 sites.

16 full hook-ups at $22.50 per night (2 people) $2.00 each additional person; $2.50 for air conditioning or electric heat). 85 sites with water and electricity - $20.50 per night (2 people); $2.00 each additional person. Campsites with water, $17.00 per night (2 people); $2.00 each additional person. Pets - no charge. Weekly, monthly, and group rates are available.

The Campground has many trees, a store for food and supplies, fish cleaning facility, laundromat, and pub which sells firewood and propane.

There are unlimited areas for walking and hiking around the lake, in the mountains and up the river.

STORES   There are stores in Lake Isabella, Wofford Heights, and Kernville. You can buy any kind of food, groceries, hardware, bait, tackle, drinks, and licenses.

MOTELS   There are motels in Lake Isabella, Wofford Heights, Bodfish, and Kernville.

GOLF   The Kern Valley Golf Course is located at the north end of the lake on the west side, just before you reach the town of Kernville. Phone (619) 376-2828.

GENERAL   Lake Isabella is under the jurisdiction of the U.S. Forest Service. It was completed in 1954, primarily as a flood control project. This function alone saves many millions of dollars annually when flood conditions exist, that would be lost by agricultural lands, oil fields, and the city of Bakersfield below the Kern River area. The lake is fed by the main fork and the south fork of the Kern River, comprising a drainage area of 2,093 square miles.

Since completion, Lake Isabella and the Kern River area (below and above the dam) have proved to be a fabulous recreation area for the fisherman, boater, hunter, hiker, golfer, and camper.

Isabella produces large fish of each kind found in the lake.

The cold water of the Kern River pours into the lake at the north and where many large trout are caught. The lake record is 9 pounds, 10 ounces for rainbow and 22 pounds, 15 ounces for brown trout.

During the Spring and Summer months, large crappie are caught by the thousands. The lake record stands at 3-3/4 pounds for crappie and 16 pounds, 15 ounces for white cats, channel cats at 22 pounds, 2 ounces.

Bluegill catches including 1 pound fish are common at Isabella. Reportedly, there was a four-pounder caught. **This is some Bluegill!!!!**

If you are a good bass fisherman, you'll get your share, as there are plenty in the lake. The record bass was caught in 1984, weight 18 pounds, 14 ounces.

A new freeway has been completed from the lake, approximately 20 miles down the Kern River Canyon. This reduces the driving time at least 20 minutes. When the freeway is completed on the lower half, it will eliminate all the sharp curves and further reduce the driving time.

If you plan a vacation, or just a day or so away from home, you can't miss by spending a few days in the Kern River Valley Area.

**Cowboy, Dave, Herschell & Jerry with
4 bass from 5 to 7.6 pounds.**

FRAZIER LAKE

This is a small pond approximately half an acre in size.

From Los Angeles take Hwy 5 over Tejon Pass two miles past Gorman to Frazier Park off-ramp. Turn left about six miles to the park.

Trout are planted periodically, and catfish and bass when available; state fishing license required. No fee for fishing. No live bait allowed and there are no fish cleaning facilities.

No boats permitted and no swimming.

There are picnic tables and a playground for children.

This is a mountain community, so there are restaurants, stores, and hotels, etc., available.

A nice Sunday drive outing – take the kids.

o o o o

MING LAKE

Ming Lake is located approximately 10 miles northeast of Bakersfield, just off Hwy 178. It is formed by the Kern River as it leaves the mountains.

The lake has 107 surface acres and is used for motor boat racing, skiing, and sailing. Sailboats allowed Tuesday and Thursday p.m. and second weekend of each month.

No minimum power boat size. Annual launching fee, $40.00; September 15 to December 31, $20.00. (Good for all Kern County lakes.)

Fishing from the bank from October through March from 8 a.m. to sundown. State regulations and limits apply.

No fee for fishing, but a state fishing license is required.

There are trout, limit 5; bass (12" size limit), limit 5; catfish, limit 20; crappie, limit 25; bluegill, no limit.

There are 50 campsites near the lake for $12.00 per night, hot showers; no hook-ups. October 16 to March 14, $8.00 per night.

No boat rentals or concession. No waders or tube fishing. No jetskis or personal watercraft.

For information, call (805) 861-2345 or Ranger (805) 872-5149.

o o o o

WOOLLOMES LAKE

Woollomes Road, Delano, CA 93215
Phones: Permit Office (805) 725-9220
Concession Office (805) 725-1004

Elevation, 321 feet   Surface Acres 300

Lake Woollomes is located approximately 138 miles north of Los Angeles. From Los Angeles take Hwy 5 north over the Ridge Route; at Wheeler Ridge bear right on Hwy 99 and go approximately 25 miles past Bakersfield to Pond Road (see Lake sign). Turn right and go 2 miles to Driver Road, left 2 miles on Driver Road to Woollomes Road, right on Woollomes Road to lake entrance.

The lake is open year round, 6 a.m. to 10 p.m. Requires a state license. There is no fishing fee.

There are no boat rentals or concessions so bring what you need with you. No motors allowed, gas or electric. Annual boat fee $40.00 (good on all Kern County lakes).

There are two paved ramps for launching with no maximum or minimum size boat. Any boat over 8' (unless propelled solely by oar or paddle) must have state CF numbers and county permit. Remember: NO MOTORS.

There are bass - limit 5 (12" size limit); catfish - limit 20; crappie - limit 25; bluegill and bullheads - no limit. Bass and crappie grow quite large. In 1976, the lake record bass was caught and it weighed 12 pounds, 4 ounces.

There are no fish cleaning facilities at the lake.

Live bait OK, including waterdogs, mudsuckers, crawfish. See Section 4.20 of California Fishing Regulations for allowable minnows. Worms, crickets, and lures OK.

There is swimming and picnicking with 30 barbeque grills, nine acres of grassed picnic areas, tables with benches, restrooms, playground equipment, drinking water, boat dock, and launch ramp.

There is no waterskiing. No wading or tube fishing.

Sailing is the predominant use as there are no motors allowed. All boats over 8' must be state registered. Inflatables - OK must have three separate air compartments and flotation device for each passenger.

No camping at present.

There are many stores in Delano, 6 miles northwest.

There are many motels on Hwy 99, approximately 6 miles from the lake.

Lake Woollomes is a 455-acre recreation area owned by the Bureau of Reclamation and operated under a lease agreement by the County of Kern. Operational jurisdiction is under the Parks and Recreation Department, 1110 Golden State Avenue, Bakersfield, CA 93301, (805) 861-2345. The primary purpose of the lake is that of an equalizing reservoir for irrigation purposes. As facilities are added, they will be reported in future editions.

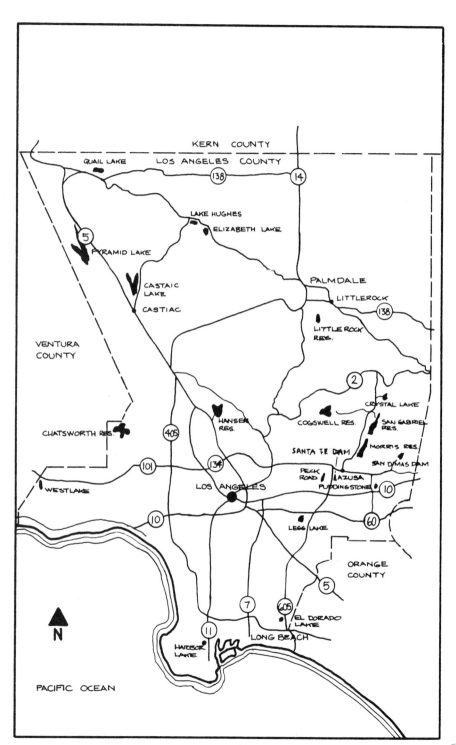

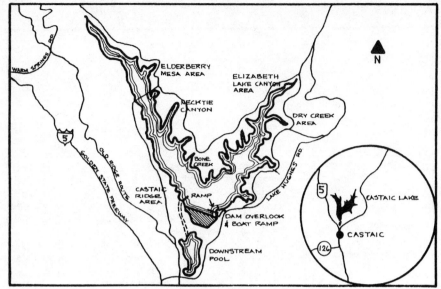

CASTAIC LAKE

32132 Ridge Route, Castaic, CA 91310
Phone: (805) 257-4050

Elevation, 1,515 feet   Surface Acres 2,230

Castaic Lake is located 45 miles north of Los Angeles on Hwy 5. Turn east off Hwy 5 in the town of Castaic. Take Lake Hughes Road to the dam overlook and the boat ramp.

OPEN & FEES
Year round, sunup – sundown, day use only. Closed Christmas. State license required. No fishing fee; auto, $6.00 per day. Summer and weekends. Good for both lakes. Annual $90.00. Senior, weekday $45.00 annual. Tube fish lower lake $6.00.

BOAT RENTALS
UPPER LAKE – (805) 257-2049
With motor: $24.00 (2 hour minimum) – plus $6.00 for each additional hour. Maximum $66.00 weekends.

BOAT LAUNCH
Two excellent multi-lane paved boat ramps. Fees: $6.00 per day, $88.00 annual, good at all times for both lakes. Annual fee of $155.00 good for boat and auto, anytime. Speed limit, 35 mph. Minimum size boat, 8 feet. Inflatables OK; must be seaworthy, over 8' and have CF number. No overnight mooring at this time.

FISH & LIMITS
Bass, 5 (min. size 12"); rainbow and brown trout, 5 combo; catfish, 10; crappie, 25; striped bass, 10 (no size limit); bluegill and bullhead, no limit. Fish cleaning at the lower lake only – none at large lake.

BAIT
No minnows allowed brought in. Waterdogs, mudsuckers, crawfish, worms, and lures OK.

SWIMMING
Yes in Afterbay Lagoon on west shore during summer months.

PICNICKING	Yes. Benches, tables, and barbeques are available, both lakes.
WATERSKI JETSKI	Yes. Sunrise to sunset – West Arm and mouth of Fish Arm only. Jetski in marked area (approximately one square mile) of upper lake every day.

SAILING – WINDSURF – Yes. In East Arm and down-stream lagoon.

MOTORBIKES Street legal. Roads only. Licensed operator.

CAMPING	Yes, on east side of the After Bay Lagoon. 58 campsites with water, no hook-ups. $12.00 per night. Reservations can be made 30 days in advance. Otherwise, first come first served. Castaic Lake RV Park – (805) 257-3340 is just east of Hwy 5 on Ridge Route Road. There is a store, laundry, heated pool, jacuzzi, and clean restrooms. 103 campsites with full hook-up, $24.00 per day; $2.00 each additional person – age 3 and over. Cable TV is free. Good Sam members welcome. Tent sites $17.00 per night.
STORES	Snack trailer at boat launch, with tackle and bait. Fisherman's Wharf, Mobile Mini Mart, and others are in Castaic where you can buy anything; licenses, ice, bait, tackle, food, drinks, and camping gear.
GENERAL	Castaic Lake Recreation Area is under the jurisdiction of the Los Angeles County Parks and Recreation Department, P. O. Box 397, Castaic, CA 91310. Phone: (805) 257-4050.

Castaic Lake is part of the Feather River Project. The dam was completed in 1971 and opened to public use in 1972.

Fishing has been fair to excellent. Trout are planted on a regular basis. A 10-pound, 4-ounce trout was caught early in 1976. Bass to 22 pounds, 1 ounce; cats to 35 pounds have been caught. Adult black and white crappie were introduced to Castaic Lake and Pyramid Lake in 1975. Largest so far is 3 pounds. Striped bass to 40 pounds, 2 ounces.

The Afterbay Lagoon is approximately 180 surface acres and provides excellent fishing for bass, bluegill, catfish, crappie, and trout. only row boats, fishing boats with electric motors, canoes, rubber rafts, sail boats with electric motors, float tubes, and wind surfboards are allowed. boat and auto fees are good on either large lake or Afterbay Lagoon. 24-hour shoreline fishing on east side of lagoon is permitted. Large picnic and parking areas as well as fish cleaning facilities provided. Tube fishing OK.

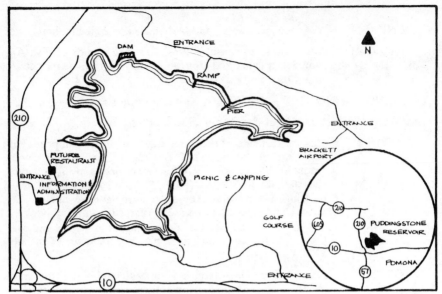

PUDDINGSTONE LAKE

Frank G. Bonelli Regional County Park
120 Via Verde Avenue, San Dimas, CA 91773
Phone: (909) 599-8411

Elevation, 940   Surface Acres 253

Puddingstone Lake is approximately 30 miles from Los
Angeles. Go east on San Bernardino Freeway to Orange
Freeway (210), north one mile to Via Verde Avenue, east on
Via Verde Park Road to lake facilities.

OPEN
Year round, 7 days per week, sunrise to 10 p.m. in the
Summer. Sunrise to 7 p.m. in Winter. Night fishing permitted
from bank until closing.

FEES
State license required. Auto permit, $6.00 per day; buses,
$20.00; RVs, 20' and over: $10.00. Age 65 and handicapped:
$3.00 per weekday excluding holidays. Annual auto is $90.00.
Senior annual – $45.00 weekdays only.

BOAT
RENTALS
Information (909) 599-2667
With motor, 4 people $34 per day, $24 – four hours
Weekends $39 per day, $27 – four hours
Jetskis for rent

BOAT
LAUNCH
Launch permit, $6.00 per day; annual, $80 unlimited use;
annual permit for boat and auto $155.00; paved ramp. Speed
limit: 35 mph. Minimum rowboat size, 8'; inflatables or
canoes, OK. Minimum motor boat size, 12' – max. 26'.

Sailboat launch on south shore Saturday and Sunday. No waders or tube fishing.

FISH & LIMITS

Bass, 5 - 12" size limit; channel cats, 10; trout, 5; crappie, 25. No limit on bluegill, red ear sunfish, and bullhead.

FISH CLEANING - There are fish cleaning facilities at the south shore.

BAIT

No minnows allowed to be brought in. Shad caught in lake OK. Mudsuckers, crawfish, waterdogs, all types of worms allowed. Bait is available at the docks.

SWIMMING

No. None in lake - Raging Waters has swimming and there are hot tubs for rent.

WATER SPORTS

Raging Waters has a 50-acre water sports complex which features wave pool with 3' swells, many different types of water slides from little ones for the small fry to the long, steep, and scary ones for the teenager. Many things for the whole family. Swimming, sun bathing, and picnicking. There are game rooms, restrooms, dressing rooms, gift shop, snack bars, and much, much more.

Raging Waters is open weekends starting in April; full time June 1 through mid-September, then weekends through October from 10 a.m. to 10 p.m. Come spend the day. For additional information, call (909) 592-6453 or (909) 592-8181.

PICNICKING

Yes. There are picnic areas for families and groups, with shelters, braisers, and restrooms.

WATERSKI JETSKI

Yes. Good water skiing, from 10 a.m. to 1/2 hour before sunset in areas as marked. Speed limit, 35 mph; maximum boat length, 26'. Jetski on odd days of the month in Summer; any day in Winter.

SAILING WINDSURF

Yes. Minimum size, 8'; maximum 26'. Special launch on south shore for sail boats.

CAMPING

There is camping for groups up to 600 with all the necessary facilities. Reservations: (800) 809-3778.

East shore: RVs - there are 400 spaces with full hook-up for $23 to $26 per night; $2.00 per person over 2 people. Be sure to call for reservations; call (800) 809-3778. Pets must be on 6' leash, $2.00 per day.

STORES

Concession and store has food, drinks, ice, bait, and most supplies; there are many stores 1½ miles north in San Dimas.

MOTELS

None at the lake. San Dimas, LaVerne, and Pomona have many. 1½ to 4 miles from the lake.

GOLF	Mountain Meadows Golf Course has been fully renovated. This is a regulation 18-hole course with a 72 par rating. Reservations may be made up to 7 days in advance: phone (909) 629-1166 or 623-3704.
AIRPORT	Brackett Field is one-half mile east on Puddingstone Drive. Phone (909) 593-1395.
HORSEBACK RIDING	Yes. Call for rentals (909) 599-8830 or bring your own horse. 1,200 acres of trails.
BICYCLES	No rentals. Bring your own bike.
GENERAL	Puddingstone Dam was built in 1928 as a flood control facility. By 1953 the County had made arrangements to purchase extra water to maintain a constant level of about 100 surface acres.

Not much more was done until 1970 when the Los Angeles County Puddingstone Reservoir (now Frank G. Bonelli) Regional Park Authority was established.

When fully completed, there will be a restaurant, family camping area, and a nature center. Total expenditures are expected to be approximately $20,000,000.

Trout plants are made regularly during the Fall, Winter, and Spring months. Many nice trout are taken in the 2 to 4 pound class. Bass to 14½ pounds have been taken, crappies to 3½ pounds, and cats to 37 pounds.

Vicente B. with his first 7 pounder – Castiac.

**John K. with two nice
Castiac crappie**

Harold C. with Castiac 6 pounder.

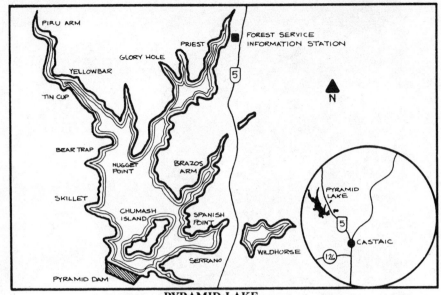

PYRAMID LAKE
Angeles National Forest
30800 Bouquet Canyon Road, Saugus, CA 91350
Phones: Gate (805) 295-1245

Elevation, 2,578 feet   Surface Acres 1,360

Pyramid Lake is located approximately 60 miles northwest of Los Angeles on Hwy 5. Take Hwy 5 approximately 24 miles past Castaic Junction to Smokey Bear Road off-ramp. Get on the west side of Hwy 5 and come back to lake on old Hwy 99.

OPEN
Year around, 7 days a week, 6 a.m. to 8:30 p.m. in the Summer; 7 a.m. to 5 p.m. in Winter. Day use only. CLOSED Thanksgiving, Christmas, and New Year's Day.

FEES
Daily parking fee $6.00 for auto, plus $6.00 per trailer; RV over 24' – $6.00. State license required.

BOAT RENTALS
Information: (805) 257-2892; Ask for Senior Discount.

	Mon thru Thurs	Fri thru Sun
Boat only:	$25 per day	$25 per day
	$20 1/2 day	$20 1/2 day
With motor:	$40 per day	$50 per day
	$33 1/2 day	$35 1/2 day

BOAT LAUNCH
There is no fee to launch your boat. Eight-lane boat ramp. 180 boat trailer parking spaces. Speed limit 35 mph – marked main body. Inflatables OK. No size limit; must be seaworthy and comply with state regulations. Slips, $10.00 per night; $50.00 per week; $75.00 per month.

A new boat ramp is being constructed at the south end of the lake. Reportedly for car-top boats and jetskis. This will be located in the Spanish Point Area. Estimated opening - Fall of 1996.

FISH & LIMITS — Large and small mouth bass - 5 (12" size limit); trout - 5; channel cats - 10; striped bass - 10; crappie - 25; bullheads, bluegill, and green sunfish - no limit. No fish cleaning facilities at present.

WADERS & TUBE FISHING - Yes, with life jacket in designated areas.

BAIT — No minnows brought in - mudsuckers, waterdogs, worms, and lures OK. No gill nets, gaffing, or spear fishing.

SWIMMING — Only one 300' beach at present, but there will be other areas developed.

PICNICKING — Ycs. 55 units at launching site. Boat-in areas with 18' x 20' ramadas are: Yellow Bar with 11, Bear Trap with 7. Spanish Point, 12 ramadas with tables and barbeque pits.

WATERSKI JETSKI — Yes, main body only - 35 mph speed limit as marked.

SAILING — Yes.

CAMPING — A new 94-unit campground has been completed (Los Alamos) by the Forest Service just 1½ miles north of the lake. There are no hook-ups or electricity, just bathrooms. No showers yet. Call (805) 248-6575 for information. $7 per night, extra vehicle, $5.00. Los Alamos campers have preference for launching their boats and jetskis.

Other facilities are at Oak Flat Camp (805) 294-8633 (8 a.m. to 6 p.m.) and Cienaga Camp (805) 296-9710. To reach these, take Hwy 5 from lake entrance back toward Los Angeles approximately 10 miles to Templin off-ramp, turn back on the old highway (south side of Hwy 5) toward the lake, go three miles to Oak Flat Camp.

Oak Flat has 27 rustic campsites for tents, trailers, campers or motor homes; first come, first served. Sites have stoves, tables, restrooms (rustic), and water. No charges.

From Templin turn-off go north of Hwy 5 approximately 5 miles to Camp Cienaga. It has 15 rustic units on a first come, first served basis - no charges. Bring your own water.

Paradise Ranch - located at Templin turn-off on the north side of Hwy 5 - has full hook-up spaces available for all types of RVs at $300.00 per month. Restrooms and hot showers also provided. For reservations call (805) 257-2728.

STORES   There is a concession (805) 257-2892, where you can buy licenses, snacks, bait, tackle, ice, and sundries. Other stores 8 miles north in Gorman.

MOTELS   There is a motel in Gorman, 8 miles north on Hwy 5 and back on Hwy 5 from Castaic to the San Fernando Valley.

GENERAL   Pyramid Lake is under the jurisdiction of the U.S. Forest Service (Angeles National Forest, 30800 Bouquet Canyon Road, Saugus, CA 91350, (805) 296-9710).

Pyramid Lake is the first large lake in the chain of lakes formed by the State Water Project which brings water by aqueduct from the San Joaquin Sacramento Delta area over 300 miles to the north.

Pyramid was opened in 1974 and fishing has been better than anticipated with catches of bass to 14 pounds, and striped bass to 40 pounds. A new trout stocking program will begin in the Fall of 1996. Small mouth bass have been planted and are doing very well in this cold water. This is a real plus for the bass fisherman.

LOS ANGELES COUNTY

Lakes not treated individually.

BIG TUJUNGA LAKE

Closed to the Public

o o o o

CHATSWORTH RESERVOIR

No Public Uses

o o o o

COGSWELL RESERVOIR

Closed to the Public

o o o o

CRYSTAL LAKE

Star Route, Azusa, CA 91702
Phones: Info (818) 335-1251
Store (818) 910-1161

Elevation, 5,600 feet   Surface Acres 7

Crystal Lake is a small 7-acre lake located in the Angeles National Forest approximately 45 miles northeast of Los Angeles. From Los Angeles take Hwy 10 to Hwy 605, north 3 miles to Hwy 210, east on Hwy 210 to Hwy 39, north through Azusa and up San Gabriel Canyon approximately 27 miles to the lake.

The lake is open year around. Summer hours: 8 a.m. to 8 p.m.; Winter hours vary.

State fishing license is required. There is a $3.00 charge for day use.

There are no rental boats. You may bring in small boats or inflatables, but must carry it in, no launching charge. Tube fishing OK.

The lake has trout - limit 5; bass, 12" size limit - limit 5; channel cats - limit 10; There are faucets at campgrounds for fish cleaning.

There is no swimming in the lake.

The store is closed at the present time (1996). There are 30 sites for picnicking at $3.00 per site.

There are approximately 176 campsites; most have water, tables, and stoves; there are modern restroom facilities. The charge is $8.00 per night on a first come, first served basis. Group campsites available. Call (818) 335-1251.

Coldbrook Campground is located 9 miles down the canyon before you get to Crystal Lake, with approximately 25 campsites at $8.00 per night on a first come, first served basis.

Crystal lake is a natural lake formed by a rock slide. This is certainly beautiful mountain country and is a worthwhile trip to take.

o o o o

EL DORADO EAST REGIONAL PARK

7550 East Spring Street, Long Beach, CA 90815
Phones:
Ranger Station	(310) 570-1765
Nature Center (8-4)	(310) 570-1745
Concession-Food-Boat	(310) 421-0884

Elevation, 55 feet   Surface Acres 30

El Dorado Park lakes are actually two lakes of 8 and 22 acres located in a 755-acre park in Long Beach approximately 22 miles southeast of Los Angeles. From Los Angeles take Hwy 5 (Santa Ana Fwy) south to Hwy 605, south on Hwy 605 to Spring Street off-ramp in Long Beach. Right on Spring Street one block to park entrance.

The park is open year around: 7 a.m. to sunset, except Christmas.

A state fishing license is required. Auto, motorcycle, and moped, $3.00 weekdays; $5.00 weekends; annual $35.00; age 60, $20.00.

There are paddle boats and row boats for rent from $7.00 to $7.50 per hour. No private boats are allowed, and no motors. Bank fishing only – no waders or tube fishing.

There are bass, limit 5 (12" size limit); channel cats, 10; trout, 5; crappie, 25; bluegill, no limit. Catfish are planted year around and trout are planted during the winter.

There are no fish cleaning facilities at the park.

No minnows allowed brought in; mudsuckers, waterdogs, crawfish, worms, and lures OK for bait.

There is no swimming. There are paved bicycle paths throughout the park and these are connected to the San Gabriel River paths. From here you can ride paved trails all the way to Whittier Narrows, some 18 miles north. There is an archery range for the archer. South of Spring Street there is a Nature Center where all types of wildlife roam free. You may see a fox, skunk, or weasel while strolling the paths. The center is open daily, 8 a.m. to 4 p.m.; closed Mondays.

There is a concession for food and boat rentals: (310) 421-0884. Open 7 days per week late June to Labor Day. Closed November, December, January, and February - other months, weekends only.

There is no individual camping - only youth organized groups. For information call (310) 570-1771.

El Dorado is under the jurisdiction of the Long Beach Department of Parks, Recreation, and Marine, 7550 East Spring Street, Long Beach, CA 90815; Phone: (310) 570-3110.

o o o o

ELIZABETH LAKE

Elizabeth Lake Road
Lake Hughes, CA 93532
Phone: Forest Service (805) 296-9710

Elevation, 3,550 feet   Surface Acres Approx. 35

Elizabeth Lake is a small, 35-acre lake located approximately 65 miles north of Los Angeles. From Los Angeles take Hwy 5 to Castaic, turn right on Lake Hughes Road, follow this to Elizabeth Lake Road. Turn right past Lake Hughes and Munz Lake to Elizabeth Lake (approximately 3 miles).

Elizabeth Lake is open year round. There is no fee and there are 21 day use sites. State fishing license required. No drinking water, so bring your own.

There are no boat rentals; there is a paved ramp for launching your boat. Boats are limited to 10 HP motors and launching is free. No jetskis are allowed.

There are bass - 5 limit (12" size limit); trout - 5; channel cats - 10; crappie - 25, bluegill and bullhead - no limit. No fish cleaning facilities. Mudsuckers, waterdogs, crawfish, and worms OK for bait.

There is no swimming in the lake, and no water skiing; sailing would be confined to small boats. Waders OK. Tube fishing OK with life vest. Windsurfing OK.

The lake is owned and operated by the U.S. Forest Service and is on a first come, first served basis. The facilities are rustic, which include tables and chemical comfort stations as well as handicap restrooms.

There are stores, motels, restaurants, gas stations within 5 miles of the lake where you can get what you need. Since it is so close, you might as well give it a try.

o o o o

HANSEN DAM
(Hansen Flood Control Basin)

11770 Foothill Blvd., San Fernando, CA 91340
Phone: Information (818) 891-0543

Hansen Dam has been closed for redevelopment and is expected to be completed and open to public use by mid 1997.

o o o o

HUGHES LAKE SHORE PARK

43667 Trail K, Lake Hughes, CA 93532
Phone: (805) 724-1845

Elevation 3,550 feet   Surface Acres 35

Lake Hughes is located approximately 60 miles north of Los Angeles. From Los Angeles take Hwy 5 north to Castaic, turn right on Lake Hughes Road; follow this to Elizabeth Lake Road; lake is around the corner on the right.

The lake is open year round. Requires state fishing license. Day-use fee for park is $7.00 per car; $1.00 each person. No fishing fee. Pets, $2.00.

There are boat rentals, $5.00 for 1 hour. Private boat use limited to small boats, canoes, inflatables, and sail boards as they must be hand carried to the lake. No charge for boat launch. NOTE: Power boats, 10 HP limit - speed limit - 5 mph.

There are bass - limit 5 (12" size limit); trout - 5; channel cats - 10; crappie - 25; bullhead, bluegill - no limit. Night fishing OK.

Mudsuckers, waterdogs, crawfish, worms OK.

Picnic tables and trees are plentiful; open fires allowed if contained. Barbeques and campfire stoves OK.

Camping rates: Approximately 60 RV spaces, some with electricity and water at $12.00 per night per vehicle. $2.00 per night for each person. Restrooms and showers. P.C.P. hikers $5.00 per night.

Sailing and swimming allowed. Waders and tube fishing OK.

Lake Hughes area, including Munz and Elizabeth Lakes, all within five miles, has upland game hunting, including deer. Hunters may get information by calling (805) 590-5126.

There are stores where you can buy anything you need. There are two motels in the area as well as restaurants and gas stations.

o o o o

JACKSON LAKE

County Road N-4, Los Angeles County
Big Pine Station: (619) 249-3504
P. O. Box 1011, Wrightwood, CA 92397

Elevation 6,000 feet   Surface Acres 7

Jackson Lake is located approximately 102 miles northeast of Los Angeles. From Los Angeles take Hwy 10 east to Hwy 15 in Ontario; go north on Hwy 15 to Cajon and intersection of Hwy 138. Go north (left) on Hwy 138 eight miles to Hwy 2; go left on Hwy 2, ten miles to Big Pines; right on County Road N4, three miles to lake.

Jackson Lake is open year round for fishing. It freezes over during winter so fishing is difficult at times. State license necessary. No fishing fee.

There are no boats for rent. You may put a small boat on, but there is no ramp and no motors are allowed. Waders and tube fishing OK.

This is primarily a trout lake (limit 5) but it does have bluegill – no limit. There are no fish cleaning facilities.

Swimming is allowed and there are tables by the beach for picnicking.

There are two tent camps: Peavine, 4 sites and Appletree, 8 sites. These have stoves, water, tables, and restrooms. Fee is $8.00 per night on first come, first served basis. There is a larger camp, Table Mountain; four miles east of the lake with 118 units that can accommodate trailers and campers at $12.00 per night.

Mountain Oak Camp, adjacent to Jackson Lake, has 22 campsites that can accommodate trailers; Lake Camp has 8 sites. Each site has tables, stoves, and water. These sites are $10.00 per night on first come, first served basis.

You may camp free during winter months at all campsites but the water is turned off.

Stores and motels are located 7 miles east, in the community of Wrightwood, where you can purchase almost anything needed.

Jackson Lake and surrounding campgrounds are under the jurisdiction of the U.S. Forest Service Valyermo District Office, P. O. Box 15, Valyermo, CA 93563; Phone: (805) 944-2187.

If you are the venturesome type, you can start on Hwy 2 in La Canada and travel the Angeles Crest Highway to Big Pines Station, then turn left 3 miles to the lake. (This route is closed during winter months.) This is truly beautiful country at 6,000 feet and above.

o o o o

LEGG LAKE

823 Lexington-Gallatin Road, S. El Monte, CA 91733
Phones: Maintenance Office (818) 575-5526
Park Superintendent (818) 575-5526
Concession (818) 575-5526

Elevation about 226   Surface Acres 77

Legg Lake is actually three lakes; approximately 39, 25, and 13 acres. Located in the Whittier Narrows Dam Recreational Area. From Los Angeles take Hwy 60 to Rosemead, south on Rosemead to Durfee, east on Durfee to lake parking on north side of street. From the east on Hwy 60, get off on Santa Anita, turn left (south), to parking area on west side of street.

The lakes are open year round from one hour before sunup to sundown.

There are no boat rentals and no concession or food and bait at this time (1996) so bring what you need with you.

There are boats for rent seven days per week, summertime and weekends and holidays during winter. No motors allowed. No private boats allowed. Also, paddle boats, aquacycles, pontoon boats, and bikes are for rent.

There are bass, 5 (12" size limit); trout, 5 (planted in winter); channel cats, 10; crappie, 25; bluegill, no limit.

There are no fish cleaning facilities.

Mudsuckers, waterdogs, crawfish, and worms OK.

There is no swimming, sailing, or skiing in the lakes. No waders or tube fishing.

The concession, (818) 575-5526, at the lake is open on weekends and holidays during school months and open 7 days per week during vacation where you can buy snacks, bait, and supplies.

The park area is under the jurisdiction of the County of Los Angeles Department of Parks and Recreation, 433 South Vermont, Los Angeles, CA 90020. Phone: (213) 738-2961 and has horseback riding, skeet and trap shooting, archery range, a hobby and picnic area, athletic area, and a nature area. This is a good place to take the kids, and the price is right! It's free!

LITTLEROCK LAKE

32700 Cheseboro Road, Palmdale, CA 93550
Phone: Store (805) 533-1923

Elevation 3,200 feet   Surface Acres 150

Littlerock Lake is located approximately 62 miles north of Los Angeles. From Los Angeles take Hwy 5 north through San Fernando to Hwy 14. Go right on Hwy 14 approximately 27 miles to Pearlblossom Hwy. Leave Hwy 14 and go right approximately 5½ miles to Four Points; right 1/8 mile to Cheseboro Road, right on Cheseboro 4½ miles to the lake.

Littlerock Lake is open year round, sunup to sundown daily. Closed Christmas. The store is open Saturday and Sunday, 8 a.m. till dark, weekdays from 9 a.m. till dark.

There is no fee to fish, just state fishing license required. Day use $3.00.

There are boats for rent, 6 a.m. – 5 p.m. (805) 944-1923. Boats only: $20.00 per 4 hours; $30.00 per day. Deposit required.

There is an unpaved launching ramp for boats; no fee for launching. There is a 5 mph speed limit on the lake, so large boats and motors are of no advantage.

There are trout – brown, rainbow and Kamloops – limit 5; catfish – 10; and bluegill and bullheads, no limit. Also good stream fishing.

No fish cleaning facilities. Waders and tube fishing OK.

Swimming is at your own risk; no lifeguards or roped-off areas. There are picnic tables at the various campgrounds in the area.

Land Management has designated an area up the canyon from the store as an OFFICIAL OFF-ROAD VEHICLE AREA for dirt bikes, four-wheelers, ATCs, and ATVs. There is a check point for your vehicle as you enter on Cheseboro Road. Be sure to check in.

There is camping at three camps (Rocky Point, Basin, and Joshua Tree) with 28 campsites that have piped water, restrooms, stoves, and tables. $7.00 per night on a first come, first served basis. There is a large area close to the store for self-contained R.V.s.

You can buy fuel, bait, groceries, and drinks at the store. There is also a cafe in the store.

The lake is under the jurisdiction of the Palmdale Water District and the Littlerock Creek Irrigation District, 35141 North 87th Street, East, Littlerock, CA 93543; (805) 944-2015. It is a good idea to call to verify the water level as it fluctuates during the year.

MACHADO LAKE
(Formerly HARBOR LAKE)
435 Neptune Avenue, Wilmington, CA 90744
Phone: Director (310) 548-7515

Elevation Approximately 20 feet   Surface Acres Approx. 80

Machado Lake is located in Ken Malloy Harbor Regional Park, approximately 20 miles south of Los Angeles. From Los Angeles take the Harbor Fwy (110) south 20 miles to Pacific Coast Hwy off-ramp, turn right one block and Harbor Lake is on the south side of Pacific Coast Highway.

The lake is open seven days per week for day use; hours vary from summer to winter.

There is no entrance or fishing fee, only a state fishing license required for people 16 years and older. Only shore fishing is allowed.

No private boats allowed at this time – 1996.

No motors are allowed and there is no fishing from rental boats.

There are catfish, limit 10; bluegill, perch and carp, no limit. See Department of Fish & Game warning on eating goldfish and carp from the lake.

There are no fish cleaning facilities at the lake.

Mudsuckers, crawfish, waterdogs, crickets, worms, and lures OK. No minnows brought in.

There is no swimming in the lake; no waders or tube fishing; just bank fishing.

There are seven youth group campsites; all have fire rings, barbeques, picnic tables, and water faucets, modern restrooms with showers and electric outlets are available. Each campsite can sleep approximately 30 people. Call (310) 548-7515 for full details.

There is picnicking with a children's play area and room to hike and loaf.

There is no concession at the lake so bring your own lunch and drinks.

Ken Malloy Harbor Regional Park is a wildlife sanctuary with many species of birds, plants, and animals. A hike around the park will provide an interesting view of many of these species.

The park is under jurisdiction of the Los Angeles City Department of Recreation and Parks, 200 North Main Street, City Hall East, 13th Floor, Los Angeles, CA 90012. Phone for information: (213) 485-5555.

o o o o

MORRIS DAM

Closed at present. Plans are to develop this for recreation when money is available.

MUNZ LAKE

Closed to the public.

o o o o

PECK ROAD WATER CONSERVATION PARK

5401 North Peck Road, Arcadia, CA 91006
Phone: (818) 334-1065

Elevation 300 feet   Surface Acres 80

Peck Road Park is located west of Peck Road in Arcadia, approximately 17 miles from downtown Los Angeles. From Los Angeles take Hwy 10 east to Peck Road in El Monte; go north on Peck Road approximately 3 miles to lake on left side of road.

Peck Road Park Lake is approximately 80 surface acres in size which is not a small pond! It is really a converted gravel pit developed by the Los Angeles County Department of Parks and Recreation, along with the Los Angeles County Flood Control District.

The lake was opened June 13, 1975. The lake is open year round from 7 a.m. to 7 p.m. May 1 to September 30 and from 7 a.m. to 5 p.m. October 1 to April 30.

There is no fishing fee - just a state fishing license required.

There are no boat rentals and no private boats allowed at this time - 1996.

The lake has bass - 5 (12" size limit); trout - 5; channel cats - 10; crappie - 25; bullhead, bluegill - no limit. There are no fish cleaning facilities at the lake. Waterdogs, crawfish, mudsuckers, worms, and lures OK.

There is no swimming, wading, camping, or overnight use of the area. No waders or tube fishing.

There is parking for approximately 200 cars; there are restrooms; tables and barbeque grills for picnicking.

The park is under the jurisdiction of the Los Angeles County Department of Parks & Recreation, 433 South Vermont Avenue, Los Angeles, CA 90020; Phone (213) 738-2961.

The Los Angeles County Flood Control District maintains the water level and is helping develop the area. This should provide many days of additional recreational use for Southern California residents - specially the kids who fish.

QUAIL LAKE

Two miles east from Hwy 5 on Hwy 138
Department of Water Resources
Phone: (805) 257-3610

Elevation 3,325 feet   Surface Acres 228

Quail Lake is located 65 miles northwest of Los Angeles. From Los Angeles take Hwy 5 north past Castaic to the Hwy 138 (four miles this side of Gorman); turn right two miles to the lake which is on the north side of the highway.

This lake is open year round - 365 days; sunup to sundown.

State license is required, but no fee for fishing.

No boats are allowed on the lake; no rentals and no ramp.

There are bass - limit 5 (12" size limit); striped bass - 5; channel cats - 10; crappie - 25; bullhead and bluegill - no limit.

There are no fish cleaning facilities in the area at present.

Waterdogs, mudsuckers, crawfish, worms, and lures OK. No minnows brought in.

There is no swimming; no motor bikes are allowed; there are no picnicking facilities and no sailing or camping. There is however, a bicycle path around the lake. There are rest stops with restrooms and small shade ramadas. Bring your own water.

There are no stores or concessions at the lake. The nearest stores are 5 miles west in the town of Gorman - so better bring what you need in the way of food, drink, and bait.

Gorman also has a motel.

Quail Lake is under the jurisdiction of the State Department of Water Resources. Local office is: P. O. Box 98, Castaic, CA 91310; Phone: (805) 257-3610.

This is the first Southern California lake in the State Water Project. It is used as a settling and regulatory reservoir for the water coming down from the North Delta Area and feeds into Pyramid and Castaic Lakes below.

Near the entrance to the lake there is a parking area for cars; you may ride bicycles or walk to the lake to fish. No other vehicles allowed.

REMEMBER: This is a primitive area, so bring what you need in the way of food, drinks, and bait.

SAN DIMAS RESERVOIR

San Dimas Canyon, San Dimas, CA 91773
Phone: Ranger (909) 593-2082

Elevation 1,470 feet   Surface Acres Approximately 35

San Dimas Reservoir is located in San Dimas Canyon approximately 35 miles east of Los Angeles. Take Hwy 10 east to Hwy 210 (Orange Freeway); turn north three miles to Hwy 30; east on Hwy 30 one mile to San Dimas Avenue; turn north half mile to Foothill Blvd., turn east one mile to San Dimas Canyon Road, turn north (left) and follow to lake.

San Dimas Canyon Reservoir is open year round. There are no fees, but you must have a fishing license. There are no facilities at the lake and no boats allowed on the lake. Parking is skimpy and the banks are almost vertical. You must hike down to the lake. No swimming, waders, or tube fishing.

There are trout - 5; channel cats - 10; and bluegill - no limit. No fish cleaning facilities. Trout are planted from November to May. This is truly rustic fishing.

There is a park with lovely picnic facilities about two miles down the canyon, close to Foothill Blvd.

If you don't like to hike and climb, pick another lake.

o o o o

SAN GABRIEL RESERVOIR

Elevation 1,453 feet   Surface Acres 250

San Gabriel Reservoir is located approximately 7 miles up Hwy 39 (north) from Azusa. It is open year round, every day.

Must have state fishing license. There are trout - limit 5; bass - 5 (12" size limit); channel cats - 10; bluegill, bullheads, and green sunfish - no limit.

The banks are very steep and it's quite a hike to get down to the lake.

There are no boats, no facilities whatsoever at the lake. Bring what you are going to use. No waders or tube fishing.

Fish are not planted here; the planted fish migrate down stream to the lake from the east and west forks of the San Gabriel River.

San Gabriel Reservoir is under the jurisdiction of the Los Angeles County Department of Public Works, 900 South Freemont, Alhambra, CA 91803. Phone: (818) 458-6106.

This is for the dedicated trout fisherman with strong legs!

SANTA FE DAM

15501 East Arrow Hwy., Irwindale, CA 91706
Phone: Fishing Information (818) 334-0713
Concession (818) 334-9049
General Information (818) 334-1065

Elevation 350 feet   Surface Acres 70

Santa Fe Dam is located approximately 21 miles from downtown Los Angeles. From Los Angeles take Hwy 10 east to the 605 Freeway; north on the 605 to Live Oak Avenue; right to Azusa Canyon Road; left (north) to lake and park.

The lake is open 7 days per week year round, 6:30 a.m. to 8:00 p.m. during the summer and 6:30 a.m. to 6:00 p.m. during the winter months.

A fishing license is required for fishing. Auto charge of $6.00 per day. Age 65 driver, or handicapped, $3.00 on weekdays. Annual pass for auto and boat available.

There are boat rentals - 12' at $8.00 per hour. Paddle boats at $8.00 per hour. You may launch your boat - $6.00 launch fee (min. 8'; max. 16') at the paved ramp on the lake. Only electric motors are allowed on the lake. Electric boats, $14.00 per hour.

The lake has bass - limit 5 (12" size limit); trout - 5; channel cats - 10; crappie - 25; bluegill - no limit. There are fish cleaning facilities at the lake. Waterdogs, crawfish, mudsuckers, worms, crickets, and lures OK.

Picnicking is on a first come, first served basis. Large family sites available for rent. There is half acre sand beaches for swimming in summer only.

There is sailing but limited to boats 8' minimum and 16' max. in length. No water skiing. No waders or tube fishing. Camping is limited to youth groups only, at present. Groups must have reservations. Phone: (818) 334-1065.

There is a concession where you can buy tackle, bait, snacks, and even an arcade with games. There are many stores and motels along Foothill Blvd. and in Azusa, two or three miles from the lake.

There are many bike trails throughout the area (bring your own bike).

Santa Fe Dam (Lake) is located inside of a large flood control dam built to contain the San Gabriel River as it leaves the mountains. Santa Fe Lake is under the jurisdiction of the Los Angeles County Department of Parks and Recreation, 433 South Vermont Avenue, Los Angeles, CA 90020; Phone: (213) 738-2961.

o o o o

WESTLAKE LAKE
Private Development

**Casitas does it again for Scott
7½ pounds.**

STATE OF CALIFORNIA
THE RESOURCES AGENCY
DEPARTMENT OF WATER RESOURCES

California Aqueduct Bikeway
ANTELOPE VALLEY

GENERAL LOCATION MAP
California Aqueduct Bikeway
ANTELOPE VALLEY

THINK SAFETY!

Don't go near the Aqueduct.
Falling in could be hazardous to health and life.
Water flow is very rapid and the concrete sides are very slippery.
Do not drink the Aqueduct water. It has not been treated.
Plan your ride according to prevailing winds and climate.

Area A

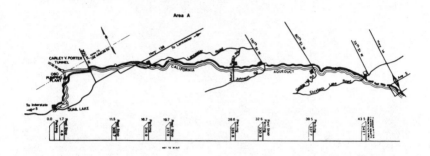

Area B

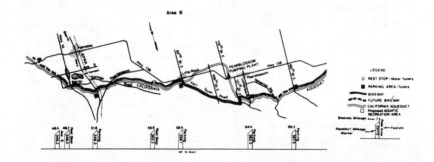

LEGEND

○ REST STOP - Water Toilets
■ PARKING AREA - Toilets
▬ BIKEWAY
▬ ▬ FUTURE BIKEWAY
═══ CALIFORNIA AQUEDUCT
□ Proposed AQUATIC RECREATION AREA

Bikeway Mileage
Aqueduct Mileage Marker ─── Feature

Area C

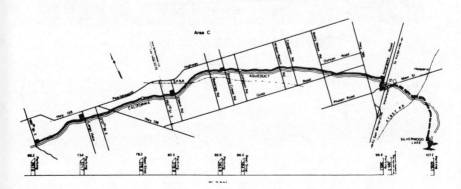

CANALS

The California Aqueduct extends some 444 miles from its origin in the Delta Region of Central California to its terminal in Riverside County. The section covered here can be reached from Los Angeles by the following routes:

From Los Angeles, take Hwy 5 north to Hwy 138 (4 miles this side of Gorman), turn right until Hwy 138 crosses the Aqueduct.

From Lancaster Road (see Area A Map) to the intersection of Elizabeth Lake Road is open to fishing; from Elizabeth Lake Road to Avenue "S" is closed. However, in this section, from 82nd Street East to 121st Street East, the canal is closed to fishing. From Valyermo to 165th Street East, the canal is closed to both fishing and bicycles. Starting at 165th Street East on to Silverwood Lake, it is open to fishing.

Another route would be, from Los Angeles, go north on Hwy 5 to Hwy 14 just north of San Fernando, right on Hwy 14 to Canal intersection just south of Palmdale (see map of Area B).

From Los Angeles go east on Hwy 10 to intersection of Hwy 15; north on Hwy 15 to intersection of Canal in Hesperia.

There are five fishing access areas that have toilet and parking facilities:
1. At the junction of Hwy 138 and 82nd Street in Littlerock - Area B Map;
2. A few miles east at the Longview Canal crossing - Area B Map;
3. Nine miles west on Hwy 138 where 77th Street crosses the Canal;
4. Just west of Hwy 14 on Avenue "S" and Canal in Palmdale - Area B Map;
5. Munz Ranch Road and Canal junction - Area A Map.

The canals are open the year around sunup to sundown.

State fishing license required. There is no fishing fee. No boats or body contact with the water.

There are bass (no size limit) - limit 5; striped bass - limit 10; cats - limit 10; crappie - 25; bullheads and bluegill - no limit.

There are no fish cleaning facilities at present; however, these are planned for all five access areas.

Waterdogs, mudsuckers, crawfish, crickets, worms, and lures OK.

There are no concessions along the canal, so bring what you need if you are cycling or fishing.

The California Aqueduct is under the jurisdiction of the State Department of Water Resources. The local office is P. O. Box 89, Castaic, CA 91310; phone (805) 257-3610.

In case of emergency, call (805) 944-1103.

NOTE: A 32-mile stretch between Hesperia and Pear Blossom has just (1996) been opened to bicycling. All other areas are closed to cycles.

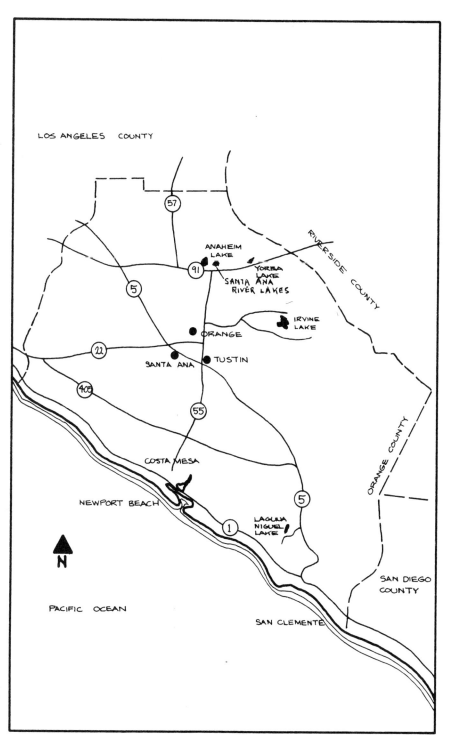

LOS ANGELES COUNTY

RIVERSIDE COUNTY

57

ANAHEIM
LAKE

YORBA
LAKE

SANTA ANA
RIVER LAKES

91

5

IRVINE
LAKE

ORANGE

22

SANTA ANA

TUSTIN

405

55

ORANGE COUNTY

COSTA MESA

5

NEWPORT BEACH

1

LAGUNA
NIGUEL
LAKE

N

SAN DIEGO
COUNTY

PACIFIC OCEAN

SAN CLEMENTE

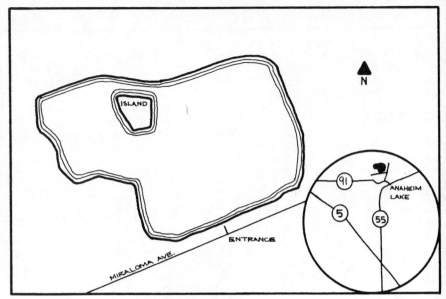

ANAHEIM LAKE

3451 Mira Loma, Anaheim, CA 92806
Phone: (714) 632-7851

Elevation, about 200 feet   Surface Acres 95

Anaheim Lake is located in the city of Anaheim, just north of the Riverside Freeway. Take Riverside Freeway to Tustin, go north on Tustin to second stop light. Turn left on Mira Loma. Anaheim Lake will be on your right.

OPEN	The lake is open year round – 6:00 a.m. to 5:00 p.m. seven days per week.
FEES	No fishing license required. Daily permits: adults, $12.00; under 12, $5.00; Under 3, free; age 62 $10.00 Monday through Friday.
BOAT RENTALS	Row boats $25.00 per day; $15.00 per half day. With motor $40.00 per day; $27.00 per half day. Monday through Thursday boats with motor $20.00 per day.
BOAT LAUNCH	Boat ramp is paved. $7.00 launching fee per day. 5 mph speed limit.
FISH & LIMITS	Trout only. Limit 5 fish. Fish planted twice weekly, Tuesday and Friday.
BAIT	No live bait, liver, horsemeat, parts of fish, or corn allowed.

FISH
CLEANING
GENERAL

There are fish cleaning facilities at the lake.

Anaheim Lake is a private lake operated by the Outdoor Safaris International; (714) 632-7851. It is STRICTLY a trout lake which is heavily stocked weekly. Management is considering catfish plants in the future.

You can drive completely around the lake and park where you want to fish.

Bait, tackle, soft drinks, and sandwiches are sold at the store. Rods and reels may be rented.

There is no swimming, water skiing, or other water sports; there is, however, a nice picnic area.

Restrooms are provided.

No pets permitted on premises.

For the beginner, or anyone wanting to relax a few hours and be almost assured of catching a fish, Anaheim Lake is the place to go. Many people catch their limit within an hour or so. The largest trout to date was a 16 pound, 2 ounce lunker.

So take the kids . . . they will love it!

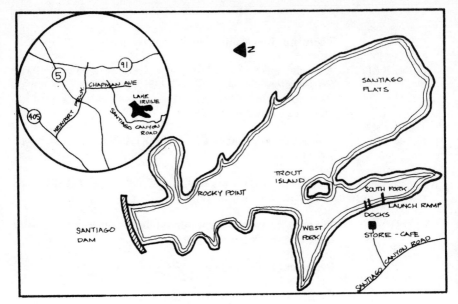

IRVINE LAKE

4621 Santiago Canyon Road, Silverado, CA 92676
Phone: (714) 649-9111

Elevation Approx. 750 feet   Surface Acres 660

Irvine Lake is located seven miles east of the City of Orange.
Take the Newport Freeway (Hwy 55) to Chapman Avenue.
Turn east, follow Chapman Avenue 8 miles to Santiago
Canyon Road. Turn right for three miles to the lake.

OPEN   Year round. June 1 through October, Sunday through Thursday 6:00 a.m. to 7:00 p.m. – Friday and Saturday 6:00 a.m. to
11:00 p.m. – November through May 6:00 a.m. to 4:00 p.m.

FEES   No license required. Day and night permits, $12.00 per adult;
$5.00 per child under 12; under 3, free. Age 62 and over,
$10.00 daily.

BOAT   Information: (714) 649-9111. No reservations taken. 100 boats
RENTALS   and motors available. No HP limit on your motor.

		Mon. thru Thurs.
Boat only, 14'	$25.00 per day	$20.00 per day
With motor, 14'	40.00 per day	27.00 per day

Pontoon boats also for rent – can reserve.

BOAT   Paved ramp. $8.00 launching fee. Boat must be 8' in length,
LAUNCH   including inflatables; 5 mph speed limit, entire lake. No HP
limit. Tube fishing – $5.00 (launch).

FISH &   Five (5) fish total (trout, catfish) plus 10 crappie, 10 bluegill;
LIMITS   sturgeon - 1. **Bass catch and release only.**

BAIT   No live bait of any kind allowed. Cut mackerel, worms, lures, and crickets OK. Powerbait is OK.

PICNICKING   Yes.

BANK FISHING - Yes. Fish cleaning facilities are provided. Tube fishing OK.

SWIMMING - SAILING - WATERSKI } NONE.
JETSKI - WINDSURF - CAMPING

STORES   The concession has a store where food, drink, bait, tackle, and supplies may be bought.

MOTELS   There are motels within 5 miles of the lake on Chapman Avenue and Santiago Canyon Road.

GENERAL   Irvine Lake is a private reservoir, managed by the P.S.A. Management Co.; Phone: (714) 649-9111.

The theory that "fishermen want to catch fish" is supported by the extensive planting schedule maintained by the operators. Fish are stocked weekly, trout in winter and channel cats in the summer. Monthly during the winter, there is an additional bonus stocking of trout from 5 to 16 pounds per fish. Large brown trout are holdovers from previous plantings.

To get some idea of the size of fish caught, the lake records are listed below:

         Bass - 14 pounds, 7 ounces;
         Bluegill - 1 pound, 14 ounces;
         Trout - 19 pounds, 5 ounces;
         Crappie - 4 pounds;
         Sturgeon - 55 pounds;
         Blue Catfish - 72 pounds, 3 ounces;
         Channel Catfish - 52 pounds, 9 ounces.

Be sure to check your large ones, you may be the next record holder!

The lake sponsors a fishing club with special discounts for admission fees, tackle, and boat rentals, with a free tournament for members. Call for information: (714) 649-9111.

Irvine's annual fishing outing for young patients of
Children's Hospital of Orange County.

Justin W. with nice 10-pound Irvine trout.

Lee P. with 52.9-pound channel catfish from
Santa Ana River Lakes.

Also lake record – Irvine Record.

ORANGE COUNTY

(Lakes are not treated individually.)

LAGUNA NIGUEL REGIONAL PARK

28241 La Paz Road, South Laguna, CA 92656
Phone: (714) 831-2791
Concession (714) 362-3885

Elevation 189 feet   Surface Acres 44

Laguna Niguel Lake is located in a 174-acre park by the same name, approximately 53 miles southeast of Los Angeles. From Los Angeles take Hwy 5 (Santa Ana Fwy) south through Mission Viejo to the Crown Valley Parkway off-ramp. Go right on Crown Valley Parkway approximately 2 miles to La Paz Road. Turn right 1/4 mile to the park and lake.

Lake is open 7 days per week from sunrise to sundown December through April – sunrise to midnight May through November. Park fee is $2.00 per vehicle weekdays, $4.00 on Saturday, Sunday, and holidays. If you fish Saturday or Sunday, concession will reduce your fishing fee $2.00. Fishing fees (in addition to park fee) are age 16 and above $10.00; under 16 years $7.00; seniors (62 and older) $8.00 per day. (Monday through Friday kids under age 18 get an after school rate of 1/2 price – $5.00.)

No state fishing license required.

There are bass and bluegill on a catch and release basis. Crappie, trout, and catfish may be kept in any combination of 5 fish total. Some nice fish have been caught – bass to 6 pounds; trout to 9 pounds, 5 ounces; bluegill to 3 pounds, 10 ounces; and cats to 49-1/2 pounds. You may fish with two poles.

No private boats allowed. 14' boats with electric motors are for rent at the concession. $8.00 per hour, $20.00 – 1/2 day – $40.00 all day.

There is NO swimming at the park. No tube fishing.

There is no camping. Picnic tables and barbeque pits are furnished in picnic areas as well as modern restrooms.

There are four tennis courts, fenced and lighted, during the summer for the tennis buff. A new amphitheater has been added.

Equestrian trails run through the park with trail tunnels passing under La Paz Road.

Dogs must be on a 6' leash.

A new lake store is open where you can buy food, drinks, tackle, and bait. Other stores are located within three miles of the lake for more elaborate shopping.

Laguna Niguel Regional Park is under the jurisdiction of Orange County Environmental Management Agency, Regional Parks Operations, One Irvine Park Road, Orange, CA 92669. Phone: (714) 771-6731.

OSO LAKE

19387 Live Oak Canyon Road
Trabuco, CA 92679
Phone: (714) 858-9313

Elevation 994 feet   Surface Acres 130

Oso Lake is located six and 7/10th miles northeast of the town of El Toro. From Los Angeles take either Highway 5 or 405 south to El Toro Road in the city of El Toro. Turn left on El Toro Road (northeast). Go 6 and 7/10th miles (7/10 mile past Marguerita Parkway) to the "OSO FISHING ASSOC" sign on right. Turn right at sign then bear left up hill to gate.

OPEN
Oso is open six days per week, sunrise to sundown. Closed on Tuesdays, Thanksgiving, Christmas, and New Year's.

FEES
Oso is a private lake with membership fees of $600.00 per year (each member must take 10 kids or more, 14 years or younger, fishing some time during the year). Guest fee is $20.00 per person per day. Children under 14 free (with member or guest). Teens 15 – 19, $10.00 (with member or guest). **Public Use Fee $40.00** per person per day. (This fee is applied once to the cost of annual membership if purchased within two months of your paid visit.)

BOAT RENTALS
Boat with electric motor $30.00 full day; boat without motor, $15.00 per half day. Call for reservations (714) 858-9313. Boat storage $25.00 per month.

BOAT LAUNCH
There are two paved ramps for launching private boats. There is no launch fee, and only electric trolling motor use is allowed. Private boats may not start their gas motors.

FISH & LIMITS
Bass, bluegill are catch and release. You may keep two catfish.

FISH CLEANING
None.

BAIT
No live bait. Stink bait for catfish OK. Red and meal worms OK for bluegill.

WADERS – TUBE FISHING – Yes.

SWIMMING   No.

PICNICKING   Yes, for paid guests.

WATERSKI – JETSKI – SAILING – WINDSURF – No.

STORES
Many stores six miles in El Toro.

CAMPING   Yes. Camping for members and youth groups.

GENERAL   Oso Reservoir was constructed in 1976 and is owned by the
               Santa Margarita Water District. The lake was stocked in 1978-
               1979 and fishing was not allowed until 1988 when the Oso
               Sportsman's Organization obtained the fishing rights to the
               reservoir. With catch and release on most fish, fishing is
               fantastic. Cats average 2 - 20 pound with the lake record at 50
               pounds. Bass and bluegill grow to lunker size as well.

               There is a clubhouse overlooking the water and a new
               amphitheater that seats over 350 people. Here many programs
               are held such as fly tying and fishing. The grounds and
               facilities are available to community and other organizations,
               for family and company picnics, weddings, etc.

               If it's a quiet, relaxing, productive fishing trip you want, try
               Oso, it's more than so-so.

NOTE: A new pond has just been built and will be stocked with large
               trout (Alper). This will be on a catch and release basis with
               only artificial lures allowed - primarily fly fishing.

               The lake is managed by the Oso Sportsman's Organization,
               19387 Live Oak Canyon Road, Trabuco, CA 92679 - Phone
               (714) 858-9313.

SANTA ANA RIVER LAKES

4060 East La Palma Avenue, Anaheim, CA 92806
Phone: (714) 632-7830; (714) 632-7851

Elevation, Approx. 200 feet   Surface Acres, Approx. 95

Santa Ana River Lakes are located in the City of Anaheim, just north of the Riverside Freeway (Hwy 91). Take Riverside Freeway to Tustin Avenue, north on Tustin one block to La Palma; right on La Palma 1/2 mile to lake entrance.

The lakes will be open January through September, Monday and Tuesday, from 6 a.m. to 5 p.m.; Wednesday and Thursday from 6 a.m. to 4 p.m. for day fishing; 5 p.m. to 11 p.m. for night fishing. Friday and Saturday from 6 a.m. to 5 p.m. day fishing, 6 p.m. to midnight for night fishing. Sunday 6 a.m. to 7 p.m. (no night fishing). Hours may vary. Closed October through December.

No State Fishing License Required.
Fees are $12.00 for adults; $5.00 for children under 12. Age 3 and under, free; Age 62, $10.00 Monday through Friday.

Santa Ana River Lakes consists of two lakes; Kids Lake, 10 acres; and Rainbow Basin, 75 acres. These lakes are stocked with 12,000 pounds of trout and catfish periodically. Five fish limit of trout and catfish, plus 10 crappie and bluegill combined. Hybrid striped bass, limit 2. All black bass caught must be released.

No live bait, no parts of fish allowed. Worms, lures, and crickets OK. Powerbait OK.

Bank fishing OK, but no waders or tube fishing.

Rental boats (714) 632-7851. Row boats - $25.00 per day, $15.00 half day; with motor - $40.00 per day, $27 half day. Monday through Thursday boat with motor $20 per day - pontoon boats available. Call about Fishing Club and discounts.

Private boats must be at least 8' in length. The ramp is paved. $7.00 launch fee. 5 mph speed limit.

No swimming, sailing, camping.

There are two picnic areas - one small and one large one where you can bring your lunch and eat between catches.

The concession has snack food, drinks, bait, and tackle. Rods and reels for rent.

The lakes are leased from the Orange County Water District, P. O. Box 8300, Fountain Valley, CA 92708 by Outdoor Safari International. Call (714) 632-7851.

These lakes are very heavily stocked so fishermen can get results for their angling efforts. Catfish to 52.9 pounds, trout to 18.8 pounds, and 7 pound bass have been caught to date. You can see from this, management means business.

YORBA LAKE
YORBA REGIONAL PARK

7600 East La Palma Avenue, Anaheim, CA 92807
Phone: (714) 970-1460

Elevation, Approx. 250 feet   Surface Acres Approx. 17

Yorba Lakes consists of four lakes located in the Yorba Regional Park which is approximately 34 miles southeast of Los Angeles. From Los Angeles take Hwy 5 (Santa Ana Fwy) south to Hwy 91 (Riverside Fwy), east on Hwy 91 to Imperial Hwy off-ramp north (left) on Imperial Hwy across the Santa Ana River to La Palma. Right on La Palma, 1 mile to the park.

The park is open 7 a.m. to 9 p.m. from April 1 to October 31; from 7 a.m. to 6 p.m., November 1 to March 1.

Entrance fee is $2.00 per entry per auto weekdays; $4.00 Saturday and Sunday; $5.00 on holidays. $50.00 annual. Seniors and disabled $12.50 annual pass. There is no fishing fee but ages 16 and older must have state fishing license.

There are no boat rentals; model boats with sails are permitted.

Since these are small lakes, no private boats are allowed.

There are bass - limit 5; catfish - limit 10; and bluegill - no limit.

There are three fish cleaning tables.

Waterdogs, mudsuckers, crawfish, crickets, worms, and lures OK.

There is no sailing, swimming, waterskiing, waders, wading, or tube fishing.

There are shade ramadas, tables, and barbeque grills for the picnickers.

There is no camping, either group or individual.

There are stores one mile west at La Palma and Imperial where you can buy anything you want.

There are bicycle, equestrian, and many hiking trails in and around the park.

There are five group shelters; and a ball diamond for the athlete. To reserve ball diamond, phone Anaheim Parks and Recreation at (714) 254-5191.

A close-in trip for the kids.

Yorba Regional Park is under the jurisdiction of the County of Orange, Environmental Management Agency, Harbor Beaches and Parks, Regional Parks Operation, #1 Irvine Park Road, Orange, CA 92669. Phone: (714) 771-6731.

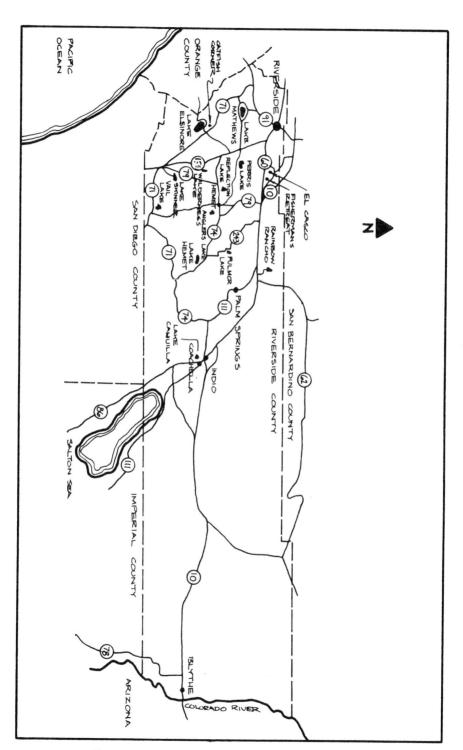

N

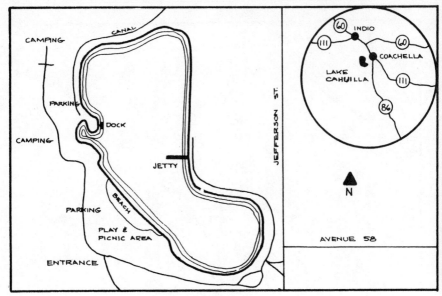

LAKE CAHUILLA

58075 Jefferson, La Quinta, CA 92253
Phone: Ranger (619) 564-4712

Elevation, sea level   Surface Acres, 135

Lake Cahuilla is approximately 130 miles southeast of Los
Angeles. Take Hwy 10 to Monroe Street near Indio. South on
Monroe to Avenue 58. Right on Avenue 58 to the lake.

OPEN   Year round – 6 a.m. to 7 p.m. Friday through Monday. Closed
                Tuesday, Wednesday, and Thursday (May to October) for day
                use and fishing during daylight savings time. Open for campers
                6 a.m. to 10 p.m. Friday and Saturday. Open to night fishing
                6 a.m. to 10 p.m. from June 1 to Columbus day, Fridays and
                Saturdays only.

FEES   Day use $2.00 adult; $1.00 child. Fishing fee $5.00 adults (16
                years and older); 6 to 16 years, $4.00; under 6 years, free.
                State fishing license required.

BOAT RENTALS – None.

BOAT   Nice boat launch. $2.00 launching fee. No gasoline motors,
LAUNCH   only electric motors, allowed; row boats, canoes, sailboats, and
                paddle boats. Inflatables must be 3-man sized; Coast Guard
                approved, one life vest per person. Tube fishing $2.00.

FISH & LIMITS	Bass, 10 (no size limit); trout, 5; cats, 10; bluegill, no limit; striped bass, 10; crappie, 25.
FISH CLEANING	None at present.
BAIT	Minnows and live bait, OK. See 1995 California Sports Fishing Regulations.
SWIMMING	Swimming pool open April through Labor Day weekend from 11 a.m. to 6 p.m. No swimming in the lake.
PICNICKING	Yes, nice tables and barbeque grills. Nice play areas for the kids.
HORSEBACK RIDING	For those who can bring their own horses, there are many miles of scenic trails. There are no rental horses. Corrals and equestrian camping available.
WATERSKI	None.
CAMPING	Groups must make reservations. Call 1-800-234-7275. There are 80 primitive campsites at $12.00 per night (no water); 10 developed campsites at $15.00 per night; and 65 campsites with electricity and water, $16.00 per night; one campsite for the handicapped. There is a dump station and showers. For reservations call 1-800-234-7275.
SAILING	Yes. This is limited only by the size of boat you can launch.
STORES	In nearby La Quinta and Coachella there are stores where you can buy anything, from 4 to 8 miles from the lake.
MOTELS	Many in Coachella and Indio, 8-10 miles from the lake.
GENERAL	Lake Cahuilla is under the jurisdiction of Riverside County Regional Parks and Open Space District, P. O. Box 3507, 4600 Crestmore Road, Riverside, CA 92519. Call (909) 275-4310.

GENERAL (continued):

Catfish are planted May through August and trout are planted during the winter from November to March which adds to the fishing fun. Catfish to 49 pounds; striped bass to 23 pounds; and bass to 14 pounds have been caught in Cachuilla, so you can see there are lunkers in the lake.

There are no gasoline motors allowed, so this is a quiet lake with no noise and only waves made by the wind. Just what a fisherman is looking for.

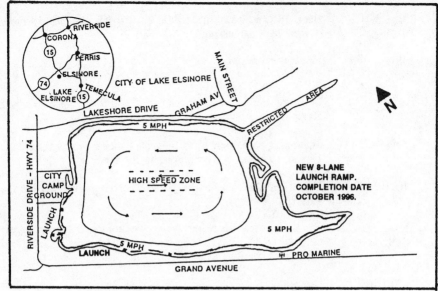

LAKE ELSINORE RECREATIONAL AREA

32040 Riverside Drive, Lake Elsinore, CA 92530
Phone: (909) 674-3177

Elevation 1,228 feet   Surface Acres Approx. 1,600

Lake Elsinore is located approximately 65 miles southeast of Los Angeles. From Los Angeles take Hwy 60 to Hwy 71 in Pomona. South on Hwy 71 through Corona to Hwy 15. South on Hwy 15 25 miles to Hwy 74 in Lake Elsinore. Right on Hwy 74 to lake and city park.

OPEN	Year round. Boating hours are: 6 a.m. to dark in the summer; 8 a.m. to 5 p.m. in winter.
FEES	State fishing license required if you fish. City park has no fishing fee. The $5.00 fee includes parking (2 persons); additional person is 50¢. Dogs are $2.00 and must be on a 6' leash. Pedestrians or bicyclists, $2.00 per person.
BOAT RENTALS	**The Recreational Area (909) 674-3177** has 13' row boats $22.50 per day, $14.50 1/2 day. Use your motor up to 15 HP (no rental motors). Paddle boards, surfboards, kayaks, floats, bicycles, umbrellas, and chairs are also for rent.

Pro Marine (909) 678-4028 at 18010 Grand (South side of lake) has 14' aluminum $45.00 per day; $22 half day. 14' aluminum with motor $69.00 per day; $38.00 half day. Pontoon and sailboats for rent as well. |

BOAT LAUNCH	Lake Elsinore West Marina at 32700 Riverside has a four-lane concrete ramp open to the public. Launch fee is $11.00 per boat which includes day use fees for 2 people, plus $3.00 for each additional person over 10 years of age. The $3.00 day use fee allows the person full use of modern restrooms, showers, as well as bank fishing. The launch fee is $9.00 for people camping at the park. Max. boat size is 30'; max. speed limit 35 mph.
NOTE:	See plans for a new 8-lane boat ramp to be built in 1996 described under the GENERAL heading on the last page of Elsinore.
FISH & LIMITS	Bass – 5 (12" size limit); catfish – 10; crappie – 25; bluegill and bullhead – no limit.
FISH CLEANING	There are no fish cleaning facilities at present.
BAIT	Mudsuckers, waterdogs, crawfish, night crawlers, and lures OK.
WADERS-TUBE FISHING	Yes. Tube fishing OK; must have personal flotation devices and stay within 5 mph buoys.
SWIMMING	Yes. Within the 5 mph buoys.
PICNICKING	Yes. Excellent facilities, $5.00 per auto with two people; 50¢ for each additional person.
WATERSKI JETSKI	Yes. Outside the 5 mph zones and designated areas. PWC operators must be 14 years or older.
SAILING WINDSURF	Yes, but it is prohibited in the fast zone.
CAMPING	**City Park:** 32040 Riverside Drive for tents, campers, trailers, and motor homes. Reservations can be made for 10 vehicles or more (909) 674-3179. All others on first come, first served basis.
	There are 200 campsites with electricity and 300 without. No hook-ups. There are restrooms and showers with hot water. Camping is $13.50 per site per vehicle per night with two people; $1.00 for each additional person. Electric hook-up, $4.00 per night extra. Dogs $2.00 per night, each.
	Lake Elsinore West Marina-RV Park: 32700 Riverside Drive. There are 200 full hook-up sites, of which 90 are available to weekenders at $19.00 per night (two people). $3.00 for extra person, limit four per site. Open camping is available, $14.00 per night (2 people). Non-campers, $3.00. Cable TV, $1.50 over night; $10.50 per week. Special weekly and monthly rates. Reservations: Call (909) 678-1300 or 1-800-328-6844.

STORES	Stores are located from half mile to 3 miles from park where you can buy anything.
MOTELS	There are numerous motels on the north side of the lake in the town of Elsinore.
AIRPORT	Skylark Airfield is located southeast of the lake, approximately 2½ miles; phone: (909) 678-4228.
GENERAL	Lake Elsinore and its camping and boat use is under the jurisdiction of the City of Lake Elsinore, 130 South Main Street, Lake Elsinore, CA 92530, Phone (909) 674-3124. The concession is operated by Lake Elsinore Recreational Area, 32040 Riverside Drive, Lake Elsinore, CA 92530, Phone (909) 674-3177.

At one time Lake Elsinore was a very flourishing resort community. However, the water inflow to the lake was erratic, sometimes floods with no storage of this water and other times near zero. With this fluctuation, the lake finally went dry in 1951. A few years back water was **purchased** to fill the lake to a reasonable level and restore the recreation facilities. There was a lake stabilization and land use plan, called "Plan C", which was being promoted by the people of the area, but in the spring of 1980 the lake was flooded from the heavy rainfall and the lake rose some 24 to 26 feet. This covered practically all the boat ramps, many residences, and property loss was so great, it is hard to estimate. Over the past two years, steps have been taken to assure good water quality by the spring of 1995. New inlet and outlet channels have been completed as well as new 19,000 linear foot levee which cuts the lake in half. Agreements have been made among the controlling agencies to maintain water level at a minimum of 1,240 feet and maximum at 1,249 feet, except during heavy rains when the water level would be allowed to reach 1,255 feet.

There has been an $800,000 grant received which will finance a new 8-lane boat launch facility at the intersection of Lakeshore and Poe Streets on the east side. Projected completion date is October 1996.

Presently, fishing for carp, crappie, bluegill, and cats is great. Bass fishing is slow due to depletion of stock and lack of spawning success. Plans are to restock bass when funds are available. It's close by, so give it a try.

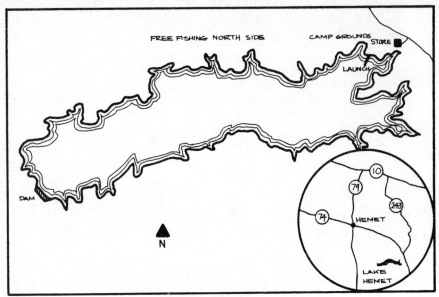

LAKE HEMET

P. O. Box 4, Mountain Center, CA 92361
Phone: (909) 659-2680

Elevation 4,500 feet   Surface Acres 420

Hemet Lake is located approximately 110 miles east of Los
Angeles, 25 miles east of Hemet in the San Jacinto Mountains.
From Los Angeles, take Pomona Freeway (Hwy 10) east
through Riverside, then south on Hwy 215 eleven miles to
Hemet turn-off, Hwy 74. Go east through Hemet on Hwy 74
for 25 miles to the lake.

OPEN   Open year round. Gates open 6 a.m.; close 10 p.m. in summer;
              winter hours – 7 a.m. to 8 p.m.; 7 a.m. to 10 p.m. Fridays.

FEES   State fishing license required. There is free fishing on the U.S.
              Forest land on the north side of the lake, from the shore only.
              If you launch or rent a boat, you must pay the day use fee of
              $7.00 per day for one car with 2 adults. Additional adults,
              $1.50 per day; children 6 to 14, 75¢. Include fishing; showers,
              25¢ for three minutes.

BOAT   Call: (909) 659-2680
RENTALS   Boat only, $7.00 per day – $5.00 1/2 day.
              With motor, $25.00 per day, $5.00 deposit. $15.00 1/2 day.

BOAT   Boat launch is not paved. Minimum size boat 10'. Maximum
LAUNCH   speed is 10 mph. Fee per day is $4.00; $15.00 weekly; or,
              $30.00 per month. This is just to leave the boat in the water,
              no slips. No inflatables, canoes, kayaks or rubber rafts.

FISH &

LIMITS	Bass - 5 (12" size limit); channel cats - 10; trout - 5; bullheads and bluegill - no limit.
FISH CLEANING	Yes. There are four cleaning facilities in the various camp grounds.
BAIT	No live minnows brought in. Mudsuckers, waterdogs, crawfish, worms, cheese, eggs, and lures OK.
SWIMMING	No. No waders or tube fishing.

MOTORCYCLES - No. Not allowed to ride in park; not even street legal.

PICNICKING	Yes. Plenty of room for this. Covered in the daily camping fee. Plenty of room to hike and walk.

WATERSKI - SAILING - No.

CAMPING   Yes. There are six dry campgrounds with 1,000 camp sites. 166 sites have electric hook-ups and approximately 160 with sewer hook-ups. All prices include camping, fishing, and showers, free dumping for those using campsites.

	DAY	WEEK	MONTH
Car: no electricity (2 adults)	$11.50	$56.00	$160.00
Car: w/electricity (2 adults)	13.75	71.75	227.50
Add'l adults (15 & over)	2.00	10.00	25.00
Children (6-14 years)	1.00	5.25	13.50
Sewer Hook-Up	1.00	5.00	15.00

STORES	Grocery store on grounds where you can buy all food, drink, camping, fishing supplies, bait, ice, and beer.
MOTELS	In Idyllwild, 9 miles north and along Hwy 74.
GENERAL	Lake Hemet is owned and operated by the Lake Hemet Municipal Water District, 40988 Florida, Hemet, CA 92543. Phone: (909) 658-3241. The lake itself is located on the Palms-to-Pines Highway in the San Jacinto Mountains at an elevation of 4,500 feet. This is a beautiful mountain meadow area surrounded by Pines, Manzanita, and Oak.

Lake Hemet produces some fine channel cats - going to 25 pounds. Bass in the 8-pound class have been caught. It is better known as a trout lake because of the suitable water and year round state trout plants. Trout from 3-4 pounds are caught regularly.

Many people enjoy the drive from Lake Hemet on Hwy 74, south and east through the mountains, down to Palm Desert and Palm Springs, then back on Hwy 10. If you enjoy the outdoors, you'll certainly enjoy the lake. This is truly a wonderful place to hike, picnic, fish, and just "laze" around.

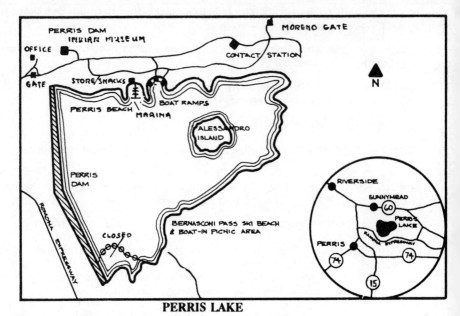

PERRIS LAKE

17801 Lake Perris Drive, Perris, CA 92571
Phones: Gate (909) 940-5603; Concession (909) 657-2179

Elevation 1,588 feet   Surface Acres 2,370

Lake Perris is located 70 miles east of Los Angeles and 80 miles north of San Diego. From Los Angeles take Hwy 60 (Pomona Hwy) east to Hwy 215, east in Riverside. South on Hwy 215 east, approximately 15 miles to the Ramona Expressway. Turn east, 3 miles to the lake.

OPEN & FEES
Year round, 6 a.m. to 8 p.m. for day use; 24 hours for campers; 6 a.m. to 10 p.m. in summer. State fishing license required. Auto fee: $6.00 per day; $75.00 per year. No fee for fishing. $1.00 per dog, per day or night. Senior, $5.00 per day use.

BOAT RENTALS
Marina (909) 657-2179, reservations; DESTINET 1-800-444-7275. Boat only - $19.00 per weekday, $23.00 Saturday and Sunday. With motor, 4 passenger - $28.00 per weekday, $19.00 - 2 hours, Saturday and Sunday $44.00 per day. With motor, 5 passenger - $33.00 per weekday, $24.00 - 2 hours, Saturday and Sunday $49.00 per day. With motor, 6 passenger - $38.00 per weekday, $29.00 - 2 hours, Saturday and Sunday $54.00 per day. 310 Slips - $9.75 per day for 9½' wide slip; $175 per month. Yearly dry storage for boats, RVs, and trailers.

BOAT LAUNCH
Excellent paved ramps - 15 lanes. Boat permit, $5.00 per day; $125 per year, auto and boat. Maximum speed 35 mph. Sail/-Paddle vessels, $5.00; sailboards, $1.00.

FISH & LIMITS
Bass (15" min. size) - 2; trout - 5; catfish - 10; crappie - 25; green sunfish, bluegill, bullhead - no limit.

FISH CLEANING	There are three cleaning stations: one at launching area; one at Perris Beach and one at east end of Mareno Beach.
BAIT	No minnows brought in. Shad caught in lake OK. Waterdogs, mudsuckers, crawfish, worms, and lures OK.
SWIMMING	Yes. Marked areas within 200 feet from shore. Wet and Wild Waterslide open during summer – (909) 657-8660.
PICNICKING	Over 300 picnic sites on the north shore with tables, ramadas, restrooms, and water; another 50 units with tables, ramadas, restrooms, and water are located on Bernacsconi Ski Beach and Alessandro Island. Groups up to 500 can be served. Write for reservations.
WATERSKI	Yes. Speed limit, 35 mph. Also, jetskiing.
WADERS	Yes. Tube fishing OK.
HORSEBACK RIDING	Yes – if you bring your own horse. No rental horses. Miles of trials. $16.00 per night for 2 at Horse Camp.
BICYCLES	10 miles of trails.
MOTORBIKE	Street legal. On roads only. Licensed operator.
CAMPING	Reservations: Call DESTINET (1-800-444-7275). Year round. 431 sites: 264 RV sites with electricity and water. (summer rates) Sunday through Thursday $21.00 per night; Friday and Saturday $22.00 per night. 167 tent sites with modern restrooms, water, and hot showers. (summer rates) Sunday through Thursday $15.00 per night – Friday and Saturday $16.00 per night. Dogs $1.00 per night each. Seniors $2.00 off. Winter rates $4.00 off each campsite. There is a regional Indian museum, "Home of the Wind" for the history buff. Admission is free for campers and day users. The museum is open 10 a.m. to 2 p.m. on Wednesdays and 10 a.m. to 4 p.m. Saturdays and Sundays. There is a campfire center where they hold evening talks on all types of outdoor subjects. Call for group rates (909) 940-5609.
HUNTING	Yes. Waterfowl; mourning doves; valley quail; jack rabbits, brush and cottontail in season. Call for specific information (909) 940-5609.
STORES	Concessions, stores, and marina have snacks, drinks, bait, gas, ice, and supplies. Numerous stores within six miles in Perris and Moreno Valley.
MOTELS	Plenty on Hwy 60, through Moreno Valley.
GENERAL	Lake Perris is under the jurisdiction of the State of California Department of Parks & Recreation, P. O. Box 2390, Sacramento, CA 95811. Local phone: (909) 657-0676. This is the last lake in the California State Water Project chain. The lake has been opened since April, 1974; the record trout weighed 7 pounds; channel cat, 30 pounds; and an Alabama spotted bass, 9 pounds, 6 ounces. Bluegill, 3 pounds, 15 ounces; Florida large mouth, 16 pounds, 8 ounces. So you see, Perris really kicks out the "big ones".

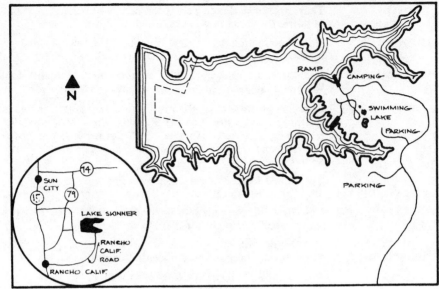

LAKE SKINNER

37701 Warren Road, Winchester, CA 92596
Phone: Gate (909) 926-1541
Store (909) 926-1505

Elevation 1,479   Surface Acres, 1,140

Lake Skinner is located approximately 90 miles southeast of
Los Angeles and 70 miles northeast of San Diego. From Los
Angeles take Hwy 60 east through Riverside, then south on
215E (395) to Hwy 74; east on Hwy 74 to Winchester Road
(79). South (right) on Winchester to Benton Road, east (left)
on Benton to STOP sign; south (right) on Buck Road to
Borrell Road; east (left) on Borrell to Warren Road entrance.

From San Diego, come north on 215E (395) to Temecula; turn
right on Rancho California Road and follow it 10 miles to
Warren Road, turn right to lake.

OPEN	6 a.m. to sunset – day use – year round.
FEES	State license required. Fishing permit: Age 16 and older, $5.00 per day; ages 6 to 15, $4.50. Adult $2.00 per day use; buses, $25 per day.
BOAT RENTALS	Information (909) 926-1505 – 4 passenger boats.

Boat only – weekdays	$15.00 per day	$10.00 – 6 hours
Weekends and Holidays	21.00 per day	16.00 – 6 hours
With motor – weekdays	27.00 per day	22.00 – 6 hours
Weekends and Holidays	47.00 per day	37.00 – 6 hours

Pontoons - weekdays	100.00 per day	67.00 - 6 hours
Weekends and Holidays	145.00 per day	95.00 - 6 hours

BOAT LAUNCH

There are two excellent paved launching ramps, $2.00 charge for launching. Boat must be at least 10' in length with 12" free board and solid decks. No kayaks, rafts, or canoes. Inflatables OK if 10' long, have 3 compartments, with floor boards and state registered.

FISH & LIMITS

Bass (12" size limit) - 5; channel cats - 10; trout - 5; crappie - 25; bluegill and bullheads - no limits. Striped bass, no minimum size - limit 10.

FISH CLEANING

Yes. In the parking lot with disposals. At Launch Ramp #1.

BAIT

No minnows. Use of waterdogs, mudsuckers, and crawfish under consideration. Worms, lures, crickets OK.

SWIMMING

Swimming pool is now open from the last Sunday in May through Labor Day. Fee is $1.00 per person per day. No swimming in lake.

PICNICKING

Yes. Can serve approximately 700 people. Group reservations, call 1-800-434-7275.

WATERSKI

No. No waders or tube fishing. No jetski.

SAILING

Yes. But sailboats must be at least 12' in length and have solid decks, no canvas, and 12" freeboard.

CAMPING

There are 260 campsites. 200 full hook-ups. Daily rates are primitive, $10.00; developed, $12.00; developed with electricity, $15.00; full hook-ups, $18.00. Family campsites are by reservation 1-800-464-7275 or on a first come, first served basis. Reservation fee, $6.50.

Group sites with electric hook-ups are $180 for up to 12 vehicles; $15.00 each additional vehicle over 12. Minimum deposit, $180.00. Full hook-ups $204.00 for up to 12 vehicles; $17.00 each vehicle over 12. Minimum deposit $204 - reservation fee $12.00. These must be reserved. Call 1-800-464-7275. There is a $4.00 charge for extra vehicles.

STORES

There is a complete campground store (909) 926-1505 that sells drinks, beer, groceries, licenses, bait, tackle, sandwiches, firewood, ice cream, and other supplies. The store does in-park catering, has bike rentals, and RV storage. Other stores are located in Temecula, 8 miles and also in Hemet, 22 miles north.

MOTELS	Nearest would be 8 miles in Temecula; many located in Hemet, 22 miles north.
HUNTING	No.
MOTOR CYCLES	Street legal and on paved roads only. Licensed operator. $4.00 per day.
HORSEBACK RIDING	No rentals as yet. Trails are primitive. Bring your own horse.
PETS	Yes. Must show evidence of vaccination and licensing. Pets must be kept on 6' leash; kept out of boats and 50' from shore. $2.00 per day per dog.
GENERAL	Lake Skinner recreation area consists of 6,000 acres owned by the Metropolitan Water District of Southern California and operated by the Riverside County Parks Department, P. O. Box 3507, 4600 Crestmore Road, Riverside, CA 92519; (909) 275-4310.

The lake was named in honor of former General Manager of the Metropolitan Water District of Southern California and was built to store Colorado River water intended for use in San Diego County.

Filling the lake began in 1973, but the lake remained closed to recreation until October of 1976. Fishing has proved quite good since the opening, producing such sizes as bass to 13-1/4 pounds, cats, 33 pounds; trout, 12 pounds, 2 ounces; crappie to 3 pounds, 9 ounces; bluegill, 1 pound, 2 ounces; and striped bass to 39½ pounds.

Many facilities are planned for the future, such as extensive campgrounds to accommodate 800 campers: 500 family, 200 groups, and 100 equestrian.

"Auld Valley Village", proposed to be moved in , is a turn of the century town composed of actual historic structures. These were present in the area during the 1800s.

A new store, restaurant, recreation room, laundromat, and gas station have recently been completed near the present camping area. This really adds to the convenience of all visitors to Lake Skinner.

The opening of Lake Skinner was certainly welcomed by all of the recreation-hungry, Southern California residents.

RIVERSIDE COUNTY

(Lakes not treated individually.)

ANGLER'S LAKE

42660 Thornton Avenue, Hemet, CA 92343
Phone: (909) 927-2614

Angler's Lake is a small, eight and one-half acre, private lake located approximately 88 miles east of Los Angeles. From Los Angeles take Hwy 60 to Hwy 215E, south on Hwy 215E twenty miles to Hwy 74, east on Hwy 74 through the town of Hemet to Soboba Street, south to Thornton Avenue to the lake.

Angler's Lake is open year round, but is closed on Mondays, except holidays.

No state license required. Day fishing fee, $11 per day for everyone; Seniors, $8.00 on Thursdays; Children 5 years to 10 years, $8.00. Under 5 years free if not fishing. No limit on the number of fish you can catch. Cats planted during summer; trout are planted during the winter months. There will be approximately 45,000 pounds of trout and cats stocked in 1996. Trout to 15 pounds and cats to 45 pounds.

No live bait allowed. There are no boats and none are allowed to be brought in.

There is all night fishing for a fee on Tuesday through Saturday – 5 p.m. to 6 a.m. from May to October.

There are fish cleaning facilities and restrooms at the lake, but no swimming. Check for tagged fish, trout have tags that are worth $5.00 to $100.00.

Camping and picnicking included in the $11.00 fee. Self-contained vehicles, tents, and trailers are welcome.

Concession has snacks, drinks, and bait. There are many stores and motels three miles away in the town of Hemet.

o o o o

A nice 50-pound channel catfish from Corona Lake.

CORONA LAKE

12510 Temescal Canyon Road, Corona, CA 91720
Phone: (909) 277-3321

Elevation Approximately 810 feet   Surface Acres 30

Corona Lake is approximately 55 miles southeast of Los Angeles. From Los Angeles take Hwy 60 to Hwy 71 in Pomona. South (right) on Hwy 71 through Corona to Hwy 15. South (right) on Hwy 15 approximately 9 miles to Indian Truck Trail off-ramp. Go left under freeway one block to Temescal Canyon Road. Turn right 1/4 mile to lake entrance.

OPEN
Open year round, 5 days per week. Closed Monday and Tuesday. Open Wednesday and Thursday from 6 a.m. to 3 p.m., Friday and Saturday from 6 a.m. to 5 p.m., day fishing. 6 p.m. to midnight for night fishing. Sunday 6 a.m. to 7 p.m. day fishing only.

FEES
No state license required. Day and night rates are same: Adults, $12; under 12, $5; age 3 and under, free. Age 60, $10. Wednesday through Friday. Club member, $10.00.

BOAT RENTALS
Boat only day or night, $25.00; 1/2 day, $15.00. Boat with motor, $40.00 all day or night; $27.00 1/2 day. Club members – $35.00 day or night; $25.00 1/2 day. Wednesdays and Thursdays boat with motor $20.00 per day.

BOAT LAUNCH
Yes. Paved ramp, $7.00 charge; 5 mph speed limit. Boat must be 8' or larger. Motorized inflatables OK. Club members, $5.00.

FISH & LIMITS
Fish limit 5 in combination of trout, catfish, and can include one hybrid bass (all other bass must be released), plus 10 bluegill and crappie in combination totaling 10 fish.

SHORE FISHING
Yes. Large area for shore fishermen. No waders; tube fishing OK. $4.00 launch for float tube.

FISH CLEANING
Yes. Very nice facilities.

BAIT
No live bait. Worms, crickets, and lures OK. No chumming allowed.

PETS
Not allowed.

PICNICKING
Yes. Tables available for picnicking; clean, modern restrooms for the public.

SWIMMING, WINDSURF, SKIING, JETSKI, SAILING, CAMPING: No.

STORES	The lake concession has snacks, food, drink, ice, tackle, and most anything a fisherman needs. Other stores along Hwy 15 for anything else you need.
GENERAL	Corona Lake is operated by Outdoor Safaris International (714) 632-7851, who also operate Anaheim Lake and Santa Ana River Lakes. All lakes are heavily stocked with trophy trout and catfish on a regular basis. Bass to 8 lbs., cats to 50 lbs., 7 oz.; trout to 16.6 lbs.; crappie to 2 lbs., 9 oz.; hybrid bass 5.8 pounds; and many nice one-pound bluegill have been caught at Corona.

Check your catch for tagged fish, these are worth various amounts of cash from $5 to $100 during contest.

Since Corona Lake is just nine miles south of Corona, it's close – take the kids.

o o o o

**Michael Kramer with
nice Corona wiper**

FISHERMAN'S RETREAT

Open to the public.
Call (909) 795-2465 for full information.

o o o o

LAKE FULMOR

Banning Idyllwild Road (Highway 243)

Elevation 5,300 feet   Surface Acres 3

This is a very small mountain lake, located approximately 100 miles east of Los Angeles; 15 miles south of Banning on Highway 243, the Idyllwild Road.

From Los Angeles go to Banning on Interstate 10; exit at Eighth Street and head south on Highway 243, go 15 miles to the lake (it is on the east side of the road and parking is on the west). Drive slowly, as you could run past the lake and miss it.

The lake is open sunrise to sunset; no charge.

The lake is stocked with trout (limit 5) by the Department of Fish and Game, so it requires the usual state fishing license.

Fulmor allows bank fishing and also has a horseshoe-shaped handicapped accessible fishing pier which extends approximately 50 feet over the water. The 1,900 square foot pier has a railing designed especially for fishing from a wheelchair.

Wader fishing is OK; no boats; no concessions; no stores, etc. You bring it all with you.

There are 36 picnic units for day use only, with drinking water, tables, stoves, and toilets – no charge.

Lake Fulmor is under the jurisdiction of the San Bernardino National Forest, San Jacinto Ranger District, P. O. Box 518, Idyllwild, CA 92549; Call (909) 659-2117 for information.

This is a beautiful mountain country. If you continue south for 10 miles or so, you reach the Idyllwild community which is a well-known mountain resort. Just the ride makes it all worthwhile.

o o o o

LAKE MATHEWS

Closed to the public

o o o o

PEPPERTREE LAKE

Closed to the public

o o o o

RAILROAD CANYON LAKE

Private development

o o o o

RAINBOW RANCHO

(Whitewater Trout Company)
Star Route 1, Box 549, Whitewater Canyon Road
Whitewater, CA 92282
Phone: (619) 325-5570

Elevation 2,350 feet   Surface One-Half Acre

Rainbow Rancho is a private trout hatchery with two small ponds open to the public. From Los Angeles take Hwy 60 east 14 miles past the town of Banning to the Whitewater cutoff. Go left up Whitewater Canyon 5 miles to the Rancho.

The Rancho is open year round. Summer - 10 a.m. to 6 p.m. Tuesday through Sunday. Winter - 10 a.m. to 5 p.m. Wednesday through Sunday.

There is an admission fee of 50¢ per person. The fishing fee is $2.50 per person. For this fee they will furnish you with pole, tackle, and bait. You may use your own tackle but it must have 10-pound test line with #8 single barb hooks. There is no license required and you may catch as many fish as you want to pay for. You are charged $2.72 per pound (1996). The fish are cleaned (25¢ per fish) for you and ready for your cooler.

The pond is stocked with one pounders and up, and the other is stocked with trout from 2 to 5 pounds. All fish caught must be kept - no releases.

Rancho caters to groups and schools for picnic, fishing, and outings. Call (619) 325-5570 for information and reservations.

There is a snack bar with munchies and soft drinks.

A trip to Rainbow Rancho is quite a surprise from the desert to a trout farm. Take the kids and bring the ice chest to haul away the trout.

o o o o

REFLECTION LAKE

3440 Cottonwood Road (at Warren Road)
San Jacinto, CA 92582
Phone: (909) 654-7906

Elevation 1,600 feet   Surface Acres 17

Reflection Lake is a small 17-acre private lake, located approximately 85 miles east from Los Angeles and approximately 6 miles northwest of Hemet. From Los Angeles take Hwy 60 to Hwy 215E, twenty miles to Hwy 74; east on Hwy 74 to Warren Road; three miles to the lake.

Reflection Lake is open year round for fishing and camping.

No state license required. Fishing fee for adults: $9.00 per day; age 6 to 15, $5 per day. This entitles you to one limit (limit is 5 trout/catfish combo); bluegill and bullheads, no limit. Children under six are free. If parked in RV site, fishing fee is $7.00.

Day use only, without fishing it is $2.00 per person. Under six is free.

There is no swimming in the lake. No waders or tube fishing.

There are 50 campsites directly on the lake front. Each site has water and electricity. Restrooms, showers with hot water, and playground are provided. Call for reservations and rates.

A store is conveniently located with all supplies such as food, drink, bait, etc. There are many stores and motels within six miles of the lake.

This is leisure fishing to be sure, but it is not a pond. Catfish to 18 pounds and trout to 5 and 3/4 pound have been caught.

So saddle up and hit Reflection Lake!

o o o o

VAIL LAKE

Is now a private development known as
Sundance Meadows Ranch
For membership information call
1-800-788-5111

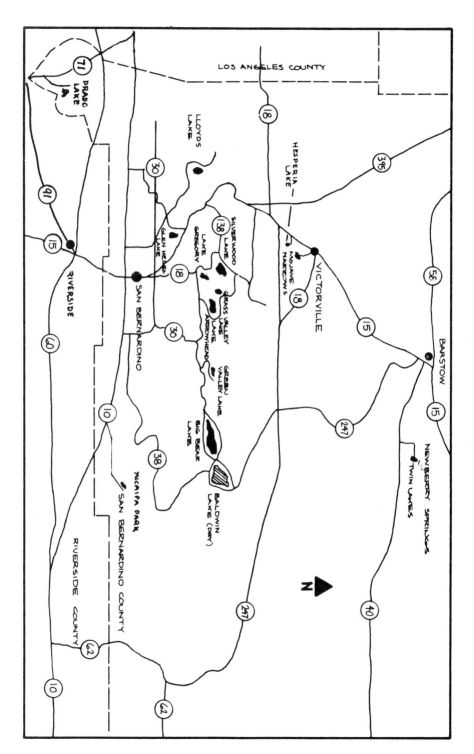

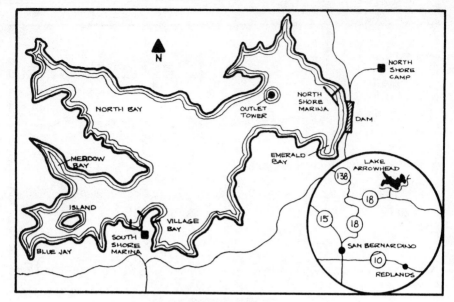

LAKE ARROWHEAD
Lake Arrowhead Marinas

P. O. Box 910, Lake Arrowhead, CA 92352
Phone: Ron's Marina, North Shore – (909) 337-9543
Chamber of Commerce – (909) 337-3715

Elevation 5,280 feet   Surface Acres 740

Lake Arrowhead is a private lake located approximately 81 miles east of Los Angeles in the San Bernardino Mountains. From Los Angeles take Hwy 10 to Hwy 15 (395). Turn north 3 miles to Hwy 18, turn right and follow Hwy 18 up the mountain 20 miles to Lake Arrowhead turn-off. Go left one mile to South Shore Marina.

OPEN	The lake is open year round; however, publish fishing is limited to the peninsula area by the Bank of America from the shore.
FEES	A state fishing license is required.
BOAT RENTAL	No boat rentals, only boat excursions from South Shore on Arrowhead Queen (909) 336-6992.
BOAT LAUNCH	Only Lake Arrowhead property owners may launch their boats; no other boats allowed.
FISH & LIMITS	Kokanee salmon and trout – 5 in any combination; bass (12" size limit) – 5; crappie – 25; bluegill and bullheads – no limit.

FISH CLEANING - There are no fish cleaning facilities.

BAIT Waterdogs, mudsuckers, crawfish, and worms OK.

SWIMMING & No public swimming or picnicking.
PICNICKING

WATERSKI Yes. For property owners and guests. No private boats. There is a ski school open to the public - (909) 337-3814.

SAILING No private sailboats allowed, and no sailboat rentals.

CAMPING There are two National Forest Campgrounds near Lake Arrowhead:

NORTH SHORE - 27 sites open weekends only. $10.00 per night; first come, first served.

DOGWOOD - Dogwood Campground is located just off Hwy 18 on the Blue Jay Road; it has 93 camp units with trailer space, water, and flush toilets, $12.00 - $16.00 per night. Reservations can be made by calling 1-800-280-CAMP from early Spring to Labor Day. From Labor Day until camps are closed it's on a first come, first served basis. For more information call Arrowhead Ranger Station (909) 337-2444 or write ARS - P. O. Box 350, Sky Forest, CA 92385.

STORES Stores close by for all supplies.

MOTELS There are several within two miles of the lake.

GENERAL Lake Arrowhead is a private lake owned by the Arrowhead Lake Association (909) 337-2595. Public use is limited to boat excursions (see Boat Rentals).

Lake Arrowhead is primarily a trout lake and is one of the few lakes where Kokanee salmon have been planted and have reproduced. These Kokes run from one to four pounds and are caught by trolling from 20 to 150 feet deep.

The fishing pressure is primarily for trout as the lake is planted year round. If you know your fishing you can do well on the crappie and bluegill as well.

The water is very clear and the trees are beautiful; this is a gorgeous Alpine Country. See it!

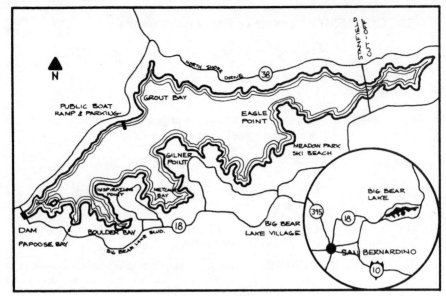

BIG BEAR LAKE

Chamber of Commerce
P. O. Box 2860, Big Bear Lake, CA 92315
Phone: (909) 866-4607

Elevation 6,750 feet   Surface Acres 3,015

Big Bear Lake is located approximately 89 miles east of Los
Angeles in the San Bernardino National Forest. Take Hwy 10
east past San Bernardino to Orange Street in Redlands (Hwy
106), turn north; go up City Creek Road, 32 miles to Big Bear
Lake.

OPEN & FEES	Year round; sunrise to sunset. State fishing license required. No fishing fee, no auto fee.
BOAT RENTALS	Boats may be rented with or without motors. Rates vary at each marina.

Boats, only: from $20.00 to $35.00 per day
With motors   45.00 to 70.00 per day

There are eight boat landings, all listed below:
1. Big Bear Marina   (909) 866-3218
2. Gray's Boat Landing   (909) 866-2443
3. Holloway's Marina   (800) 448-5335
4. Lighthouse Trailer Park   (909) 866-9464
5. Pine Knot Landing & Marina   (909) 866-2628
6. Pleasure Point Boat Landing   (909) 866-2455
7. North Shore Landing   (909) 878-4386
8. Captain John's Fawn Harbor and Marina   (909) 866-6478

Larger boats, ski boats, sailboats, jetskis, windsurfer, and canoes also available. Call for further information and reservations.

BOAT LAUNCH — All boats launched on Big Bear Lake must not exceed maximum length, 26'; the speed limit is 35 mph; all manual operated boats under 12' must stay in the 5 mph zone.

There are two public paved ramps (free launch). Both are on the North Shore. One is approximately two miles from the dam (Phone: (909) 866-2917); and the other is approximately 8 miles from the dam on the east end of the lake (909) 866-5200. The Lake Patrol Offices are located next to both ramps.

Most of the marinas have ramps where you can launch for a small fee.

Day rates for all vessels are $15.00 per day. Annual permits are $65.00 for all state-registered craft, and $25.00 for all non-registered vessels such as row boats, canoes, kayaks, and other manually operated craft. 62 or older, $10.00 discount annually.

If you desire further information on boating rules and regulations, call Big Bear Municipal Water District (909) 866-5796 or Public Ramp (909) 866-2917.

FISH & LIMITS — Bass – 5 (12" size limit); cats – 10; trout – 5; crappie – 25; bluegill – no limit.

FISH CLEANING — There are fish cleaning facilities at some of the boat landings and campgrounds. Some motels also have facilities for cleaning fish.

BAIT — No minnows brought in. Waterdogs, mudsuckers, crawfish, and worms OK.

SWIMMING — Yes. Waders and tube fishing all within 50 feet of shore.

PICNICKING — There are numerous campgrounds around the lake for picnicking – also, many areas for hiking.

WATERSKI – JETSKI – Yes – as marked – 35 mph speed limit.

SAILING — Yes. Also windsurfers permitted.

HUNTING — Dove, duck, and deer in season. Check closed and open areas with the Big Bear Ranger Station: (909) 866-3437 before making the trip.

MOTORBIKES — Street legal, in most cases, with proper spark arresters for back roads.

HORSEBACK RIDING	Rancho Ose Grande - (909) 585-3604; Magic Mountain Stables (909) 878-4677.
GOLF	Bear Mountain Golf Course (909) 585-8002 - 9 hole, 2,800 yards, par 32.5.
CAMPING	There are at least five improved public campgrounds in the Big Bear Lake area. Serrano and Pine Knot are close by. There are three more from 3 to 14 miles from the lake.

Holcom Valley (no charge and no water), Big Pine Flat, and Hana Flat all have trailer spaces but only Serrano has showers and 30 RV hook-up spaces, plus 102 primitive sites. Reservations can be made for 50% of the sites at Serrano, Pine Knot, and Hana Flat. The other 50% of the sites are on a first come, first served basis. All sites at Holcom Valley and Big Pine Flat are on first come, first served basis. For reservations, call 1-800-280-2267

For further information call Forest Supervisor's Office (909) 383-5588 or Big Bear Ranger Station (909) 866-3437.

RV and Trailer Camps
1. Big Bear Shores RV Resort - (909) 866-4151 - sites for motor homes, travel trailers, and fifth wheelers.

2. Holloway's RV Park - (800) 448-5335 - 99 sites. Full hook-ups $25 to $35 per night.

3. Lakeview Pines Trailer Park - (909) 866-2230 - 76 sites, full hook-ups. 26 RV sites, 50 mobile home sites - $20.00 per day, $100 per week, $300 per month.

4. Lighthouse Trailer Park, North Shore - (909) 866-9464.

5. Big Bear M.W.D. RV Park - (909) 866-5796 - 21 full hook-ups: $25 per night; 4 primitive sites: $15 per night; modern restrooms and showers. On South Shore. Special rates by the week or month.

STORES	There are many stores on both North and South Shores where you can buy anything you want.
AIRPORT	Yes. Big Bear City Airport (909) 585-3219. It is between Hwys 18 and 38 at the east tip of the lake.
MOTELS	There are numerous motels around the lake. A few are listed here:

1. Bavarian Lodge	(909) 866-2644
2. Embers Lodge	(909) 866-2371
3. Fireside Lodge	(909) 866-2253

4. Golden Bear	(909) 866-2010
5. Goldmine Motel (Moonridge)	(909) 866-8786
6. Henry's Cottages and Motel	(909) 866-2526
7. Marina Riviera Motel	(909) 866-7545
8. Moore's Motel	(909) 866-4804
9. Robinhood Inn & Lodge	(909) 866-4643
10. Smoke Tree	(909) 866-2415
11. Thunder Cloud Lodge	(909) 866-7594
12. Wishing Well Motel	(909) 866-3505

PRIVATE RENTALS

Private cabins and homes, any size, can be rented by calling Big Bear Reservations Service, Phone (909) 866-3671 or Big Bear Central Reservations, Phone (909) 866-4601 or First Cabin Resort Reservations, (909) 866-9689.

GENERAL

Big Bear Lake is owned and operated by the Big Bear Municipal Water District, P. O. Box 2863, Big Bear Lake, CA 92315, (909) 866-5796; however, the boat landings and facilities are privately owned.

Big Bear has long been a much-used recreation area for the people of Southern California. Excellent hunting, fishing, hiking, and skiing are jut a few of the attractive activities available for the visitor.

Fishing in the past has been mainly for trout. The businessmen plant trout in addition to the regular plantings of the Department of Fish and Game. These are usually in the one-pound class. The largest was 14 pounds, 11 ounces.

During the past few years, Florida bass have been planted and have grown to 8 and 10 pounds; also, large channel cats to 28 pounds have been caught.

Big Bear Valley and the surrounding area has a very lively and colorful history. Gold was discovered here in 1860 by Bill Holcomb, and all that follows gold discoveries happened here, including horse thieves and hangings. So, if you are interested in early California history, you'll have a field day in this area.

There is an alternate way to get to Big Bear that is longer, but certainly a worthwhile drive through scenic mountain country. Take Hwy 10 to Redlands, then east on Hwy 38, up through the Barton Flats area and across the upper reaches of the Santa Ana River and approach Big Bear from the southeast side. For different and contrasting scenery, you can return to the southern basin by taking Hwy 18 east past Baldwin Lake, down on the Mojave Desert to Lucerne Valley, on to Victorville and back on Hwy 15.

A trip to Big Bear gets you away to another world. Take the family . . . it's great!

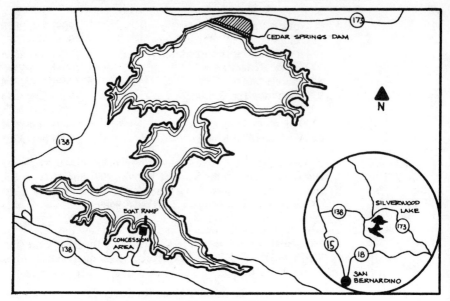

SILVERWOOD LAKE

14651 Cedar Circle, Hesperia, CA 92345-9799
Phones: Gate (619) 389-2303
Marina (619) 389-2320
Information (619) 389-2281

Elevation 3,378   Surface Acres 995

Silverwood Lake is located 85 miles east of Los Angeles and 30 miles north of San Bernardino on the north side of the San Bernardino Mountains. From Los Angeles, take the San Bernardino Freeway, Hwy 10 to Hwy 15 in Ontario. North (left) on Hwy 15 to Cajon Junction. Turn right on Hwy 138 approximately 11 miles to lake and recreation entrance.

OPEN The park is open year round – day use only (camping areas, 24 hours).

SUMMER – April 1 through September 30 – 6 a.m. to 9 p.m.
WINTER – October 1 through March 31 – 7 a.m. to 7 p.m.

FEES State license required. No fishing fee. Car passes: $6.00 per day; $75.00 per year. Age 62 and over, $5.00 per day.

BOAT
RENTALS
No reservations taken for fishing boats. No row boats. Must have your motor or rent one.

14' or 16', your motor	10 hours, $19.00 weekdays
	10 hours, $23.00 weekends
15' with 8 HP	10 hours, $33.00 weekdays
	10 hours, $49.00 weekends

Winter rates are discounted. Gas included with motor rental. 10-passenger pontoon boats for rent.

BOAT LAUNCH	There is an excellent paved ramp for boat launching and parking area for 175 cars and trailers. (Trailers must be removed from the parking lot each night.) Boat fee per day is $5.00; $50.00 per year. Non-power boat, $2.00. NOTE: No boat launch after September 15, 1996, due to drawn down. Projected re-open April 1997.
FISH & LIMITS	Bass (12" size limit) – 5; trout – 5; channel cats – 10; striped bass – 10; crappie – 25; no limit on bluegill and bullheads.
FISH CLEANING	Excellent fish cleaning facilities with conveyor disposer. Probably the most modern in existence.
BAIT	No minnows brought in. Waterdogs, mudsuckers, worms, crickets, lures, and crawfish OK.
MOTOR CYCLES	Street legal only. On roads – no trails. Operator must have license.
SWIMMING & TUBE FISHING	Yes. In designated areas with lifeguards. Daily in summer. Waders and tube fishing OK in restricted area with Coast Guard approved life jacket.
PICNICKING	Yes. Family picnic sites throughout the area with piped drinking water, barbecue grills, sanitary facilities. Parking for over 600 autos. Additional picnic sites are located at the Chamise, Live Oak, and Sycamore Landing areas. These sites can only be reached by boat and you must bring your own supplies, including drinking water. No open fires, cook stoves, or barbecues permitted in the area.
WATERSKI JETSKI	Yes. In designated areas, 6 a.m. to sundown in summer, 7 a.m. to sundown in winter. Speed limit 35 mph.

SAILING – WINDSURF – Yes. No limit on size. Must be seaworthy.

BICYCLING	Bring your own. There are 13 miles of trails in the park.
CAMPING	There are 136 individual campsites at $17.00 per night Sunday through Thursday; $18.00 per night Friday and Saturday May 1 through October 31. Seniors $2.00 discount. November 1 through April 30, $8.00 per night.
	Each site is paved for two cars and has tables with cupboards, barbecues, restrooms and hot coin-operated showers are available. No hook-ups. There is a 10-day stay limit from June 1 to September 30; otherwise the limit is 30 days; 8 people per campsite.
	There are 7 back-pack and bike campsites at $3.00 per person, per night that share the same facilities. Full facilities for the handicapped. Disabled Discount Pass Program honored.

12 Noon is check out time.

For reservations: Call DESTINET: 1-800-444-7275. Must be made at least 2 days before and up to 7 months in advance. RESERVATIONS ARE A MUST DURING SUMMER!

Group Camping – There are 3 group campsites; each will accommodate from 10 to 100 people and up to 30 cars. Reservations: DESTINET 1-800-444-7275.

Smaller group sites 10-80 people, $80.00 per night. Call (619) 389-2281 for reservations.

Other camping is approximately 9 miles north of the lake at Mojave River Forks on Hwy 173; (619) 389-2322

STORES   Concessions at boat ramp and on swim beach have snack bars for food, drink, bait, fishing, and other supplies. Groceries can be purchased in the stores five miles from the marina.

MOTELS   Nearest in Crestline and Hesperia – 10 to 17 miles.

GENERAL   Silverwood Lake is under the jurisdiction of the State of California, Department of Parks and Recreation, P. O. Box 2390, Sacramento, CA 95811.

The lake is formed by the Cedar Springs Dam (249') located on the north side of the San Bernardino Mountains. This is the highest lake of the State Water Project Aqueduct System and has storage capacity of 24 billion gallons. This water comes over 400 miles through seven pumping plants to provide Southern California with much needed water.

Trout, bass, and catfish were planted early on and are doing well. Trout to 12 pounds, 4 ounces; bass to 16 pounds; and cats to 15 pounds have been caught. Since the water comes from river sources in Central California, other species will come with the water. There have been a number of striped bass caught to 55½ pounds (March, 1996), which were definitely not planted. The Department of Fish and Game has planted Sacramento perch to see if they will reproduce and add to the fishing fun. This could prove interesting.

SAN BERNARDINO COUNTY

(Lakes not treated individually)

BALDWIN LAKE

Elevation 7,100 feet   Usually Dry

Baldwin Lake is located about 4 miles east of Big Bear Lake on the east edge of Big Bear City.

The lake is normally dry and therefore does not offer anything to the fisherman. Mention is made here because it bears the name of one of the very colorful historic figures of Southern California during the 1800s, "Lucky" Baldwin.

The Lucky Baldwin Mine is just about 1½ miles north of the lake. Those who enjoy plodding through historic areas will have a great time in this valley.

There are no plans for developing recreational facilities and there are no fish in the lake other than minnows.

o o o o

CUCAMONGA GUASTI REGIONAL PARK

800 North Archibald Avenue, Ontario, CA 91761
Phone: (909) 481-4205

Elevation, 952 feet   Surface Acres 11 Total

Cucamonga Guasti Regional Park has two small lakes: one is approximately 4 acres and the other is 10 acres. The park is located approximately 45 miles east of Los Angeles. From Los angeles take Hwy 10 east approximately 4 miles past Ontario to Archibald Avenue, north on Archibald approximately ½ mile to the park.

The park is open from 7:30 a.m. to dusk 6 days per week year round, except it is closed Wednesdays, Thanksgiving, Christmas, and New Year's Day.

Auto fee, $5.00; pedestrians, $2.00. State fishing license is not required. Trout plantings October to April each year. Fishing fee is $5.00 for everyone 8 years and older; under age 8, $2.00. Annual auto fee, $75.00; age 62 and disabled, $55.00.

Paddle boats are rented during summer months. No private boats or motors allowed.

There are channel cats – 5; trout – 5. Trout are planted from November to April each year, including some trophy sized fish.

There are no fish cleaning facilities at the park. No waders or tube fishing.

Mudsuckers, waterdogs, crawfish, worms OK for bait.

There is swimming – $2.00 per person, ages 4 and over. There is a two-flume, 230-foot water slide at $4.00 for five rides, or $8.00 per person for all day swimming and slide use.

Picnic sites throughout the park have tables and barbeques.

Bring the kids so they can use the modern playground equipment provided for their enjoyment.

There is a snack bar and bait store available at the park. Many stores in the surrounding area.

Cucamonga Guasti Regional Park is under the jurisdiction of the San Bernardino County Regional Parks Department. For more information, call (909) 387-2594 or (909) 945-4321.

o o o o

GLEN HELEN LAKE

2555 Devore Road, San Bernardino, CA 92407
Phone: (909) 880-2522

Elevation 1,870 feet   Surface Acres Total 13

Glen Helen Lake is located approximately 60 miles east of Los Angeles, one mile from Hwy 15. From Los Angeles take Hwy 10 three miles past Ontario to Hwy 15, turn left (north) on Hwy 15 to Sierra Avenue off-ramp. Go left one half mile on Sierra Avenue to Devore Road, turn right on Devore Road and go about three miles to the park.

Glen Helen actually has two lakes; one of 3 acres, the other of 10 acres at the base of the San Bernardino Mountains.

The park is open 7:30 a.m. til dusk; year round, seven days per week, except closed Christmas.

You must have a state fishing license. Entrance fee is $5.00 per day per car. $2.00 per pedestrian. The fishing fee is $5.00 for everyone 8 years of age and older; under 8 years, $2.00. One limit per person per day consists of 5 trout and 5 catfish. No limit on bluegill.

Mudsuckers, waterdogs, crawfish, worms OK for bait. There are no fish cleaning facilities.

There are pedal boats for rent, $5.00 per half hour. No fishing boats or private boats allowed – just bank fishing. No waders or tube fishing.

There is a one-half acre swimming complex with two flumes, 350-foot waterslides, snack bar, and children's playground. Swim fee (4 years and older) $2.00 per person; waterslide, 5 rides for $4.00. All day swim and slide, $8.00.

Excellent set up for picnic and barbeques.

Group camping for 10 or more. Call (909) 880-2522. Individual camping is available but no hook-ups. There is a dump station for RVs.

There is a concession and snack bar; larger stores are approximately 10 miles away.

Glen Helen is a San Bernardino County Regional Park. If you want to get away for a day, or maybe a weekend, this is just a short trip from the Los Angeles Basin.

○ ○ ○ ○

GRASS VALLEY LAKE

Closed to the public

○ ○ ○ ○

GREEN VALLEY LAKE

Green Valley Lake, CA 92341
Phones: (909) 867-2009
Chamber of Commerce (909) 867-2411

Elevation 7,200 feet   Surface Acres Approx. 20

Green Valley Lake is located in the San Bernardino Mountains, approximately 73 miles east of Los Angeles. From Los Angeles take Hwy 10 to Orange Avenue in Redlands; turn north to Hwy 30; follow Hwy 30 up through Running Springs, four miles to Green Valley Lake turn-off; turn left and go 4 miles to the lake.

Green Valley Lake is a small, private lake, open Spring through Fall. There is a small fee for fishing and swimming. State license required. Fish cleaning facilities available.

Row boat, $5.00 per hour; $15.00 - 4 hours; $25.00 - 8 hours. No motors allowed. Paddle boats, canoes, and kayaks available. No private boats allowed. Boats available from Spring through October 31.

There is picnicking and swimming and lots of hiking area.

The lake is planted with trout, 2 to 13 pounds, with 5 limit; cats - limit 5. Small mouth bass - 5 limit. Record trout caught was 13.52 pounds.

Camping one mile from lake at Green Valley Lake Campground: 37 sites at $10.00 per night; two-thirds of the sites may be reserved by calling 1-800-280-2267, the remaining one-third are first come, first served (909) 337-2444. There are cabins and cottages for rent. Call (909) 867-3534 and (909) 867-4522.

LAKE GREGORY

P. O. Box 656, Crestline, CA 92325
Phone: (909) 338-2233

Elevation 4,520 feet   Surface Acres 120

Lake Gregory is located in the San Bernardino Mountains approximately 72 miles east of Los Angeles and 14 miles north of San Bernardino. From Los Angeles take Hwy 10 east to Hwy 15 and Hwy 395. Turn north 4½ miles to Hwy 18, follow Hwy 18 for eleven miles to the top of the mountain. Turn left three miles to the lake.

The lake is open from the last Saturday in April to the third Sunday in October: 7:00 a.m. to 5:00 p.m. daily. Weekends open 6:00 a.m.

State license required. No auto fees – and bank fishing is free on east side from one hour before sunup to one hour after sunset, year round.

Boats are rented for $5.00 per hour, 2 hour minimum, $25 deposit. Only electric motors are allowed (no gas motors) and only private sailboats allowed from Memorial Day to Labor Day. Size minimum, 7'8" length; $5.00 per day. Paddle boards and aqua cycles also for rent during the summer.

There is bass, limit 5; channel cats – 5; trout – 5; crappie – 25; bullheads, no limit. There is a new fish cleaning facility with disposer. No live bait is allowed. Record trout was 11½ pounds, June 1995.

Swim beach and water slide open Memorial Day weekend through Labor Day weekend, $30.00 season swim pass, or $3.00 per day (4 years and older); 5 ride water slide, $4.00. Swim admission and all day water use, $9.00. Age 62 and the disabled, Season Pass, $20.00; family season pass (4 people), $65.00. Areas available for picnicking.

There is no waterskiing, no wading. Tube fishing is OK. $5.00 launch fee.

The nearest camping is Camp Switzerland: (909) 338-2731 (private); tents, $17.00 per night; RV, $20.00 per night with hook-up.

There are stores within walking distance of the lake where you can buy food, drinks, ice, snacks, and supplies.

There are many motels in the area:
Sleepy Hollow Cabins	(909) 338-2718
North Shore Motel	(909) 338-5230
Moon Lodge	(909) 338-7375

Lake Gregory is approximately 6 miles west of Lake Arrowhead and one mile from Crestline in the San Bernardino Mountains. It is a short drive from the City of San Bernardino (14 miles) and the setting is beautiful . . . nestled in the mountains, with large pine trees. It is worth the trip, just to drive past and continue down the mountains from Crestline, 10 miles to Silverwood Lake, then continue west on Hwy 138 to Hwy 15 in Cajon Pass. Makes a good Sunday drive.

HESPERIA LAKE PARK

7500 Arrowhead Lake Road, Hesperia, CA 92345
Phone: (619) 244-5951

Elevation 3,200 feet   Surface Acres 7

From Los Angeles take Hwy 10 east to Hwy 15. Left (north) on Hwy 15 up over Cajon Pass to Main Street. Right on Main Street to Arrowhead Lake Road to Lake Park. 9 miles from Highway I-15.

OPEN
The lake, park, and store are open 365 days per year. Day fishing, year round; night fishing, May – September.

FEES
No fee for park. Fishing fee: $5.00, adults; $2.50, age 15 and under. Seniors, 20% discounts on Monday and Tuesday. No state fishing license required.

BOATS
No rental boats and no private boats allowed.

FISH & LIMITS
The lake has bass, trout, catfish, crappie, and bluegill. Limit is any combination of 5 fish. Trout is stocked weekly, October through April. Catfish stocked, May through September. Catfish to 15 pounds; trout to 8 pounds.

BAIT
No live bait allowed. Worms, cheese, salmon eggs, and lures OK.

SWIMMING – WATERSKI – HUNTING – SAILING – None.

PICNICKING
Yes. Tables, barbeques, and fire rings as well as group sites available. Playground for youngsters. Horseshoes, open pitching. Bird watching and also an equestrian area.

CAMPING
Yes. Approximately 53 sites for trailers, campers, and tents, with water faucets throughout this area, $12.00 per night; with electric hook-up, $15.00 per night. There are modern restrooms with hot showers. Call for group rates.

STORES
There is a store (open 365 days per year) where you can buy bait and tackle, ice, camping and fishing supplies, drinks, and hot and cold food.

GENERAL
Hesperia Lake Park is under the jurisdiction of the Hesperia Recreation & Park District, P. O. Box 401055, Hesperia, CA 92845. Phone: (619) 244-5488.

o o o o

JENKS LAKE

Elevation 6,700 feet   Surface Acres 5

Jenks Lake is a small mountain lake located approximately 89 miles east of Los Angeles in the San Bernardino Mountains. From Los Angeles take Hwy 10 through San Bernardino to Hwy 38 (Orange Avenue) in Redlands. Turn north one mile to Hwy 38. Turn right and follow Hwy 38 thirty-one miles to Jenks Lake Road right on Jenks Lake Road approximately two miles to the lake.

The lake is open for day use only from May through September.

There is a $5.00 parking fee – state fishing license required. There are trout (limit 5), bass (limit 5), catfish (limit 10), bluegill (no limit). Trout are planted regularly from June through September.

There are no boat rentals and only small boats, inflatables, and canoes are allowed . . . with no motors. No fee for launching. Tube fishing OK.

There is swimming, picnicking, and hiking at the lake.

There are four campgrounds within a short distance of the lake for camper trailers, RVs, and tents. South Fork has 23 sites at $8.00 per night. Heart Bar has 94 sites at $8.00 for singles and $16.00 for doubles per night. Both areas have water and vault toilets. Barton Flats has 47 sites and San Gorgonio has 60. Both have been renovated and include new picnic tables, wider spurs, flush toilets, and hot showers at $10.00 to $20.00 per night. Reservations (BIO-STHERICS 1-800-280-2267) can be made for all campsites except South Fork, which is on a first come, first served basis. Barton Flats has a dump station available to the general public not staying at campgrounds for a $3.00 fee.

There is a store, service station, and restaurant at Camp Angelus (Angelus Oaks) approximately 8 miles west of the lake where you can buy any kind of supplies needed from gas to drinks and groceries.

The lake is under the jurisdiction of the U.S. Forest Service Mill Creek Ranger Station, 34701 Mill Creek Road, Mentone, CA 92359; Phone (909) 794-1123.

This is a delightful drive up Highway 38 which is the back door to Big Bear Valley. It is truly one of the scenic areas of our Southern California Mountains.

o o o o

JESS RANCH – ANGLING POND
11401 Apple Valley Road, Apple Valley, CA 92308
Phones: (619) 240-1106; (619) 247-5299
CLOSED AT PRESENT

MOJAVE NARROWS PARK

P. O. Box 361, Victorville, CA 92392
Phone: (619) 245-2226

Elevation 3,200 feet   Surface Acres 30

Mojave Narrows Park is located approximately 100 miles northeast of Los Angeles. From Los Angeles take Hwy 10 to Hwy 15 in Ontario. Turn north over Cajon Pass to Bear Valley cut-off (4 miles this side of Victorville), go east 4 miles to Ridgecrest Road; north (left) three miles to park.

Mojave Narrows actually has two lakes: Horseshoe and Pelican. Horseshoe is 20 acres and Pelican is 10 acres.

The park is open 6 days per week year round from 7:30 a.m. to sunset, except Tuesdays and Christmas. Entrance fee is $4.00 per vehicle (family) per day weekdays, $5.00 weekends and holidays. Pedestrians, $2.00 per person. Age 62 and Disabled, $45.00 annually.

State fishing license required. Combined fishing and entrance fee, $8.00 per weekday and $9.00 per day weekends. Seniors combined fishing and entrance fee, $4.00 with pass. Dogs, $1.00 per day, must be on leash.

Row boats may be rented. $5.00 per hour; minimum 2 hours. Paddle boats are also available. No private boats. Only electric motors allowed.

You are allowed bass, 5 (12" size limit); trout, 5; channel cats, 5; no limit on bluegill. There is one fish cleaning facility.

No swimming allowed; there are grills, tables, and shade for picnickers. No waders or tube fishing.

There are 38 full hook-up sites for trailers, campers, and motor homes at $15 per night. 22 additional sites (primitive) have water every 3 sites. These are $10 per night (tents OK). Seniors $8 per night, Sunday through Thursday. There are modern restrooms and hot showers. There are 10 group areas for 10 to 100 vehicles, $50 minimum plus $10 for each vehicle over 10. Reservations by phone or write the park. Call (619) 245-2226.

There are many trails for hiking in the woods and along the stream (Mojave River). Horses for rent, $10.00 per hour. Hayrides are a scheduled activity.

There is a snack bar and bait shack where you can buy snacks, drinks, and some supplies, as well as bait; mudsuckers, waterdogs, crawfish, worms, and lures are OK for bait. Other stores would be in Victorville, about 7 miles away.

The park is under the jurisdiction of the San Bernardino County Regional Parks Department. For more information, call (909) 387-2594 or (619) 245-2226. You will find this park a complete surprise in the middle of the desert, where you are expecting nothing but cactus and sagebrush.

PRADO REGIONAL PARK

16700 South Euclid, Chino, CA 91710
Phone: (909) 597-4260

Elevation 555 feet   Surface Acres 56

Prado Park is located 43 miles east of Los Angeles. From Los Angeles take Hwy 10 (Pomona Fwy) east to Hwy 71 in Pomona; right on Hwy 71 approximately 9 miles to Euclid Avenue, left on Euclid Avenue to Prado Park.

From beach cities take Hwy 91 to Hwy 71, three miles to Euclid Avenue, right on Euclid to park.

Prado Park is open year round, 7 days per week; 7:30 a.m. to dusk for day use. Closed Christmas.

Entrance fee is $5.00 per car for day use. Pedestrians, $2.00. If you fish, you must have a state license. A fishing fee is charged: $5.00 for anyone 8 years and older, under 8 is $2.00.

There are row boats for rent at $4.00 per hour, 3-hour minimum, weekdays; and $7.00 per hour weekends. Paddle boats, $5.00 per half hour per boat.

There is a paved ramp where you may launch your small boat up to 16', but it must be solid hull (no inflatables or rubber rafts permitted). The launching fee is $2.00; canoes OK; electric motors OK. No gas motors allowed.

There are trout, limit 5; channel cats, 5; bluegill and bullheads, no limit.

There are no fish cleaning facilities at the lake.

No minnows brought in. Mudsuckers, waterdogs, crawfish, crickets, worms, and lures OK.

There is no swimming at present. No waders or tube fishing.

There are 100 plus acres for picnicking, with tables and barbeques.

There is sailing but no catamarans allowed and the boat must be 16' or less in length. No waterskiing. No jet skis.

Motor bikes must be ridden on paved roads by licensed operator and be street legal. $5.00 entrance fee.

There are riding stables where you can rent horses. Weekends only in winter. Many miles of trails.

There are three softball fields and five soccer fields. Make reservations for these, call (909) 597-4260.

There are two 18-hole golf courses located across the street [El Prado (909) 597-1753] and a skeet shooting and dog training facility close by at 17505 South Euclid, (909) 597-4794. Dogs must be on a leash. $1.00 per dog per day.

There are 50 sites with full hook-ups at $15 per night. Overflow area for self-contained vehicles, $5.00 per night; maximum stay five months in any six-month period. Group areas with hook-ups $11.00 per night per site, plus $10.00 group reservation fee. Group tent sites for 1 to 50 people $3.00 per person; 51 and more, $2.00 per person per night. Call (909) 597-4260.

There is a snack bar and store where you can buy bait, ice, charcoal, snack foods, drinks, and supplies. There are many stores and motels within 5 miles of the park.

Prado Regional Park (2,000 acres) is under the jurisdiction of the San Bernardino County Regional Parks Department, 825 East Third Street, San Bernardino, CA 92415, (909) 387-2594.

∘ ∘ ∘ ∘

YUCAIPA REGIONAL PARK

33900 Oak Glen Road, Yucaipa, CA 92399
Phone: (909) 790-3127

Elevation 2,860 feet   Surface Acres 20

Yucaipa Regional Park has three regularly stocked lakes and is located approximately 79 miles east of Los Angeles, near the town of Yucaipa. It is surrounded by the San Bernardino and San Gorgonio Mountains. From Los Angeles take the San Bernardino Fwy (Hwy 10) east approximately 4 miles past the town of Redlands to the Yucaipa Blvd. off-ramp. Go left on Yucaipa Blvd. approximately 6 miles to Oak Glen Road; left on Oak Glen Road 2 miles to the park.

The park is open daily 7:30 a.m. to dusk. Closed for Christmas.

Day use fees are: $5 per car and $2 per pedestrian. If you fish the fee is $5 per person, 8 years and over; under 8, $2.00. If you are 16 years or over, a state fishing license is required (a book of fishing permits available at discount rates). There is a fee of $1 per dog and must be on leash. Age 62 and Disabled: Annual fee is $55.00. Under age 62 annual pass, $75.00.

$5.00 is required for all motorbikes. Must be street legal, ride on paved roads only by duly licensed operator.

The lakes are stocked with catfish, limit 5; and trout, limit 5 in season. There are no fish cleaning facilities.

No minnows brought in. Mudsuckers, waterdogs, crawfish, crickets, worms, and lures OK.

Paddle boats and aqua cycles are for rent from Memorial Day to Labor Day (no other boats). No waders or tube fishing.

Swimming is great ($2.00 fee) in the one-acre swim lagoon which has sandy beaches and a 350-foot water slide you can use for a fee of $4.00 for 5 rides; $8.00 all day.

There are beautiful picnic sites that rise above the lakes with shade structures, tables, and barbeques for individuals as well as groups.

There are 26 paved sites for RV camping. Hook-up sites are $15-$17 per night. Other primitive sites are $11.00 per night with 4 water outlets for this area. $11.00 tent sites also available; Seniors $8-$15 Monday thru Thursday. There is a snack bar where you can buy snacks, drinks, bait, ice, and some supplies.

There are many stores and motels within five miles of the park in the town of Yucaipa and along Highway 10.

Yucaipa Regional Park is under the jurisdiction of the San Bernardino County Regional Parks Department, 825 East Third Street, San Bernardino, CA 92415; Phone (909) 387-2594.

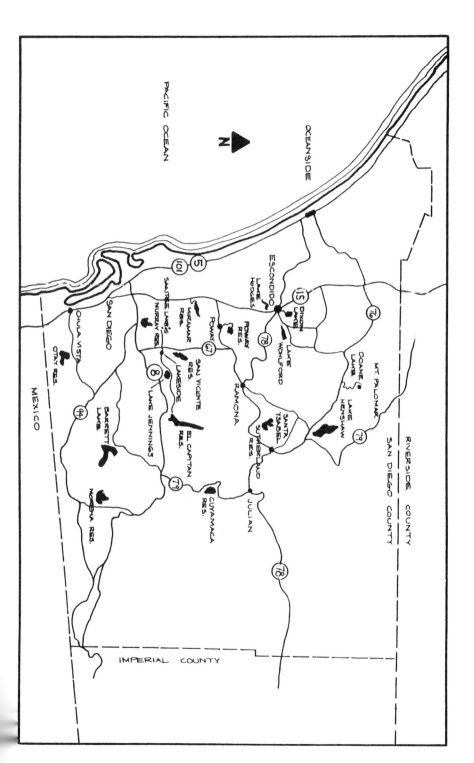

-115-

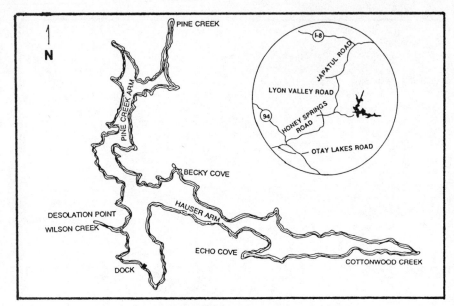

BARRETT LAKE

Phone: (619) 668-2050

Elevation 1,607   Surface Acres 811

There are two ways to reach Lake Barrett. Go south on 805 Fwy to Hwy 94; east on Hwy 94 through Jamul to Honey Springs Road; left on Honey Springs Road 7.7 miles to Lyon Valley Road. Right on Lyon Valley Road 1.7 miles to gate on the right; through gate approximately 3 miles to lake.

The second route, going east on Interstate 8, turn right on Japatul Road 5.6 miles south to Lyon Valley Road, left on Lyon Valley Road 6 miles to gate that is located just past mile post #12. Left through gate approximately 3 miles to lake.

NOTE: The gate is kept locked and is opened only for those holding valid permits.

OPEN   The lake permits are on a lottery basis. For information about entering the drawing call (619) 668-2050. For permit holders the lake is open sunrise to sunset Wednesday, Saturday, and Sunday, April through September by lottery drawing only.

FEES   State fishing license required. Adults, $4.00 per day; ages 8 through 15, $2.00 per day.

BOAT   Boat only $8.00 per day; $6.00 1/2 day
RENTALS   With motor   25.00 per day; 20.00 1/2 day

BOAT LAUNCH – No private boats.

FISH & LIMITS	Bass are on a catch and release basis only; barbless hooks. Crappie - 25; bluegill and bullheads - no limit.
FISH CLEANING	None at present.
BAIT	Artificial lures with **barbless** hooks only. Red and meal worms may be used for bluegill.
WADERS	Yes. Tube fishing OK.
PICNICKING	Yes, for permit holders.

WATERSKI - JETSKI - SAILING - WINDSAIL - CAMPING - No.

HUNTING	Yes. Waterfowl. Open mid-October through mid-January Wednesdays and Saturdays till noon.
MOTELS	Many 10-15 miles from lake.
GENERAL	Barrett Lake is under the jurisdiction of the City of San Diego Water Utilities Department, 5540 Kiowa Drive, La Mesa, CA 91942; Phone (619) 668-2050.

o o o o

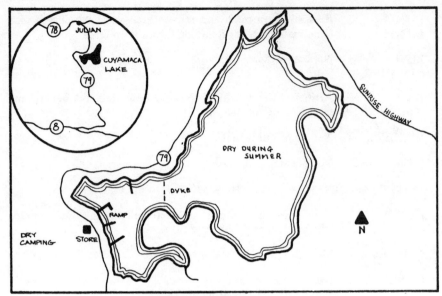

LAKE CUYAMACA

15027 Highway 79, Julian, CA 92036
Phone: (619) 765-0515; 447-8123

Elevation 4,700 feet   Surfaces Acres 110 Summer level

Lake Cuyamaca is located approximately 160 miles southeast
of Los Angeles and 51 miles northeast of San Diego. From
Los Angeles take Hwy 5 south to Carlsbad; go east on Hwy 78
through Escondido and Ramona to San Ysabel. Right on Hwy
78, 7 miles to Julian. Turn right on Hwy 79, 9 miles to the
lake. From San Diego, east 40 miles on Hwy 8 to Hwy 79; turn
north on Hwy 79, 11 miles to the lake.

OPEN	Year round, sunrise to sunset.
FEES	State fishing license required. Adults, 16 and over, $4.75 per day; ages 8 through 15, $2.50 per day; ages 7 and under no charge if accompanying adult pays to fish.
BOAT RENTALS	No reservations, first come, first served. Boat only $12 per day, $10 per half day With motor 25 per day, 20 per half day
BOAT LAUNCH	Paved ramp for launching, $3.00 per day. No annual fee. Maximum length, 18'; minimum, 10'. Speed limit 10 mph. Canoes and inflatables, OK. See page 178.
FISH & LIMITS	Bass – 5 (no size limit); trout – 5; channel cats – 5; bluegill and crappie – 25 each. Excellent fish cleaning facilities. No small-mouth bass to be possessed.

BAIT	Golden and red shiners (no other minnows allowed), water-dogs, mudsuckers, crawfish, crickets, worms, & lures OK.

SAILING – SWIMMING – WATERSKIING – No. Monday through Friday waders and tube fishing OK

PICNICKING	Yes, on the island shore. Excellent hiking.
HUNTING	Duck hunting in season. Call (619) 765-0515.
MOTORBIKES	Street legal, on roads only.
HORSEBACK RIDING	Yes. One stable, 30 minutes from the lake. For the horseman there is Los Caballos Camp. Open mid-May through November 1 with 16 campsites, each having 2 pipe corrals. You can bring 2 horses per campsite at $19.00 per weeknight, $20.00 Friday and Saturday night. $2.00 for each additional horse. There is also day use.
CAMPING	75 RV spaces at lake campground. 24 have water and electricity, $17.00 per night. Dry camp and tent sites, $12 per night. There is a dump station and 14 tent sites.
	Nearby Cuyamaca State Park (2½ miles south of lake) has a total of 166 campsites for tents, RVs, and trailers up to 27' at $15 per weeknight, $16 Friday and Saturday nights, one vehicle. Extra vehicle $5.00. Dogs $1.00 each – must be on 6' leash. There are restrooms, coin-operated hot showers. For reservations call MISTIX 1-800-444-7275; March 31 through October 31. For additional information: (619) 765-0755. Seniors (62 and up), $2 off camping; $1 off day use. Reduced winter rates.
STORES	Lake Resort has store and snack bar for bait, tackle, food, drinks, supplies, and licenses; also, restaurant and gas station. Other stores 9 miles in Julian.
MOTELS	Nearest would be nine miles in Julian or 11 miles to Hwy 8. Lakeland Resort on south shore has cabins, (619) 765-0736.
GENERAL	Lake Cuyamaca is operated by the Lake Cuyamaca Recreation and Park District, 15027 Hwy 79, Julian, CA 92036.

Since the lake is located at the 4,700' level, it supports trout fishing year round. Plants are made four times per month during summer which provides excellent trout fishing. Trout to 14 pounds, 1 ounce have been caught in Cuyamaca. Catfish to 22 pounds are caught by true catfishermen. The bass record stands at 13-3/4 pounds and bluegill at 2 pounds, 4 ounces.

This area is rich in Indian lore and truly beautiful mountain territory. Gold was discovered in the area around 1870 and considerable mining was done in the surrounding mountains.

A drive through this area is very rewarding to the eye even if you don't throw a hook in the water. Take the family . . . you'll be glad you did.

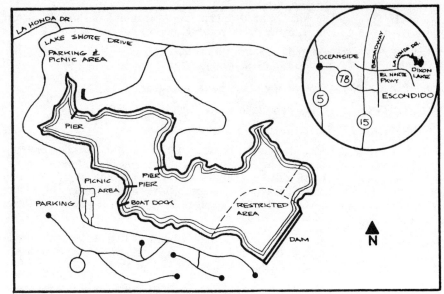

DIXON LAKE

1700 North La Honda Drive, Escondido, CA 92025
Mailing Address: 201 North Broadway, Escondido, CA 92025
Phones: Ranger Station (619) 741-4680
Concession (619) 741-3328

Elevation 1,045 feet   Surface Acres 70

Dixon Lake is located approximately 105 miles southeast of Los Angeles. From Los Angeles take Hwy 5 south to Oceanside. Turn east on Hwy 78 to Hwy 15 in Escondido; left on Hwy 15 one-half mile to El Norte off-ramp. Right (east) on El Norte to La Honda Drive; on La Honda Drive to lake.

From San Diego come north on Hwy 15 to El Norte off-ramp in Escondido; right on El Norte to La Honda Drive, left on La Honda to lake.

OPEN   Seven days a week, year round; 6 a.m. to dusk; night fishing during summer months. Call (619) 741-4680 for information. Closed Christmas.

FEES   State fishing license required. $1.00 per car, van, or motorcycle, day use weekends, no charge during week; over 60, free. Fishing: $5.00, adults; $3.00, 8 through 15 years; under 8, free; over 60, $4.00.

BOAT   No reservations, first come, first served.
RENTALS   Boat only $10 per day; after 1 p.m. $8 – 1/2 day
            With motor   18 per day; after 1 p.m. 14 – 1/2 day
            No gasoline motors allowed. You may bring your own electric motor and battery. Night rates same as half day.

BOAT LAUNCH - No private boats allowed.

FISH & Bass, 5 (12" size limit); trout, 5; channel cats, 5; crappie, 5;
LIMITS bluegill are catch and release; red ear sunfish, no limit. Fish
caught by children under 8 count against adult's limit. Excellent fish cleaning room.

BANK FISHING - Yes. Also three piers. No waders or tube fishing.

BAIT Golden and red shiners (no other minnows allowed), waterdogs, mudsuckers, crawfish, crickets, worms, & lures OK.

SWIMMING - SAILING - WATERSKIING - No.

PICNICKING Yes. Three picnic areas of rolling grass and shade trees with
barbeques and picnic tables. Some sites have shelters with
electricity. Fees: $1.00 per car, van, or motorcycle; buses, $3.00
day use. Many trails for hiking and nature walks.

MOTORCYCLES - Street legal - on paved roads only. Licensed operator.

CAMPING 45 campsites with tables, stoves, and lockers are available for
overnight use. Ten have utility and sewer hook-ups for trailers
and RVs. Full hook-ups $16 per night; other $12 per night; $2
second vehicle. RESERVATIONS: Can be made by phone
Monday through Friday at Concession between 8 a.m. and 4
p.m. Phone: (619) 741-3328. Walk-in reservations can be made
at Lake Concession, 8 a.m. to 4 p.m. Monday through Friday.
No pets allowed in the park.

STORES There is a concession where you may purchase licenses,
permits, bait, tackle, food, beverages, and supplies. Many
stores in Escondido, 2 to 3 miles south.

MOTELS Many in the city of Escondido, south of the lake.

GENERAL Dixon Lake Recreation Area consists of 527 acres of park with
hills, trails, camping areas, and a 70-acre lake, operated by the
Escondido Public Works Department, 201 North Broadway,
Escondido, CA 92025; (619) 741-4691. The lake was stocked
with fish in 1971 but was not opened to the public until May
12, 1977. Florida bass have been caught to 16 pounds, 12
ounces; trout to 12 pounds, 2 ounces; cats to 24 pounds, 6
ounces; and red ear sunfish to 3 pounds, 8 ounces. Trout are
planted through winter months and add much to the fishing
fun. Catfish planted during summer months.

There are three fishing piers around the lake for shore
fishermen; one is equipped for handicapped persons. Over 60
cards available at 201 North Broadway, Escondido.

Dixon Lake is nestled in the hills north of Escondido and is a
treat awaiting your visit.

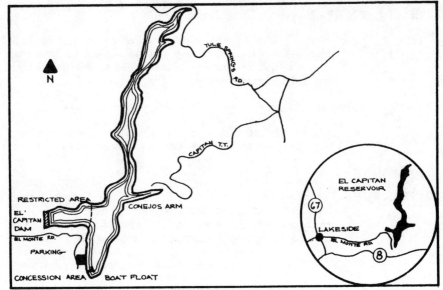

EL CAPITAN LAKE

Lakeside, CA 92040
Phone: (619) 668-2050

Elevation 750 feet   Surface Acres 1,574

El Capitan Lake is located 30 miles north and east of San Diego. Go east on Hwy 8 to Lake Jennings Park Road; north to Lakeside; east on El Monte Road, 8 miles to lake.

OPEN	Sunrise to sunset, year round; February to late September open Friday, Saturday, Sundays, and holidays. October through January – open Saturday and Sundays and holidays.
FEES	State fishing license required. Adult permit, $4 per day; 8 to 15 years, $2; under 7, free. Waterski and jetski $5 adults, $2.50 juniors.
BOAT RENTAL	Reservations: (619) 390-0222; Monday through Friday, 9 a.m. to 5 p.m. Boat only $ 8 per day; $ 6 half day With motor 25 per day; 20 half day
BOAT LAUNCH	$5 per day. Paved ramp for launching. Maximum speed, 35 mph; no maximum HP. Canoes and kayaks, OK. Inflatables; See Section on Inflatables.
FISH & LIMITS	Florida bass, 5 (15" minimum size); channel and blue cats, 5; crappie, 25; red ear sunfish, bluegill, no limit.

FISH CLEANING	There are no fish cleaning facilities.
BAIT	Golden and red shiners (**no other minnows allowed**).
WADERS	Yes. Tube fishing OK.
PICNICKING	Yes.
MOTORBIKES	Street legal – paved roads only.
WATERSKI JETSKI	Yes. In marked area only.
SAILING	Yes, including catamarans. No sinks or toilets.
CAMPING	Tents and trailers at nearby Lake Jennings County Park. Call (619) 565-3600.
STORES	Food and beverages, bait, tackle, permits, and licenses may be purchased at Lake Concession which is open February through September. Other stores at nearby El Monte County Park.
MOTELS	Many in Lakeside, El Cajon, and along Highway 8.
GENERAL	El Capitan Lake is under the jurisdiction of the city of San Diego Lakes Recreation Program, Water Utilities Department, 5540 Kiowa Drive, La Mesa, CA 91942. Phone for information (619) 668-2050.

El Capitan Lake is under the jurisdiction of the city of San Diego Lakes Recreation Program, Water Utilities Department, 5540 Kiowa Drive, La Mesa, CA 91942. Phone for information (619) 668-2050.

Florida bass were planted in El Capitan along with the other San Diego City Lakes. These bass have grown well here; the lake record of 15 pounds, 5 ounces proves the point. During the spring months great number of large crappies are caught, many in the 3-pound class. The record channel cat weighed 21 pounds, 6 ounces; blue cat, 45 pounds, 5 ounces.

Red ear sunfish and bluegill also thrive in this lake, which adds to the fishing fun. If you are a fisherman you will do well here.

Twenty-four hour fishing information: (619) 465-FISH.

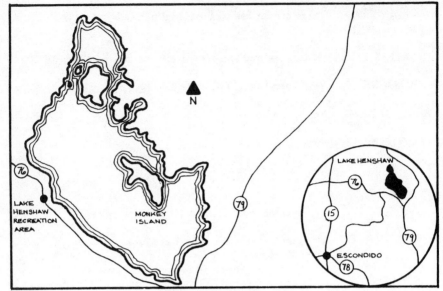

LAKE HENSHAW

Santa Ysabel, CA 92070
Phone: (619) 782-3501

Elevation 2,740 feet   Surface Acres 1,334

Lake Henshaw is approximately 120 miles southeast of Los
Angeles by way of Hwy 71 to I-15, on to Hwy 76, then east to
lake, and approximately 139 miles by way of Hwy 5 to Hwy 76
in Oceanside, then east to lake. It is approximately 60 miles
northeast of San Diego.

OPEN	Year round, seven days per week. Most of the year, 6:30 a.m. til sundown.
FEES	State fishing license required. Lake day use permit $5.00 age 13 and older; age 12 and under, free when accompanied by paying adult. Pets $1.00 per day.
BOAT RENTALS	Information: (619) 782-3501 Boat with motor $30 per day, $25 after 1 p.m.

BOAT LAUNCH – Free; minimum size 10'; speed limit, 10 mph. No canoes, kayaks, or sailboats.

FISH & LIMITS	Large mouth bass – 5 (12" size limit); channel cats, bullhead cat, 10; crappie – 25; bluegill – 25. Excellent fish cleaning facilities in RV park. Covered area with light.
BAIT	Waterdogs, mudsuckers, crawfish, crickets, worms, and lures OK. Wader fishing, OK. No tube fishing.

SWIMMING	Swimming pool and therapy pool for registered guests. No swimming in the lake.

SAILING - WATER SKIING - None. No jetski. No motorbikes.

HUNTING	Call (619) 782-3501 information. Goose and duck.
PICNICKING	Yes. Near the trailer park across road from the lake. Also, excellent hiking.
CAMPING	Year round basis. First come, first served. Information (619) 782-3487.

RV - Trailers
100 spaces with full hook-up for trailers, $16.00 per day; $96 per week; $220 monthly. Dump station on site, $2.00 charge.

Camping
Located next to the trailer park. Contains modern restrooms, dozens of picnic tables, and more than 100 camping sites. Four persons per car, $14 per day; $1.00 for each additional person over 5 years, under 5 years, free. Pets $1.00 per day.

CABINS	17 housekeeping cabins equipped with dishes, linens, utensils, refrigerator, stove, and heat; from $45 to $56 per day, depending on the cabin and the number of persons. Reduced weekly rates.
STORES	The resort store has the basic foods, bait, fishing tackle, etc. There is a restaurant serving a wide selection of food, soft drinks, and beer.

GAS STATION Nearest is 11 miles - so bring your own gas.

MOTELS	None nearby.
GENERAL	Lake Henshaw was constructed by William G. Henshaw in 1922 to supply water to communities of Vista and Escondido.

The lake was stocked in 1926 with crappie, bluegill, bass, and catfish. Since then, the fish have thrived under the balanced conditions found in the lake, making it one of the truly outstanding fishing lakes in the world.

Record catches are: bass, 14 pounds, 10 ounces; channel cats, 39 pounds, 8 ounces; crappie, 2 pounds, 14 ounces; bluegill, 1 pound, 10 ounces; bullhead cat, 2 pounds, 3 ounces.

Concessions and recreation facilities are owned and operated by the Lake Henshaw Resort Inc. (619) 782-3501.

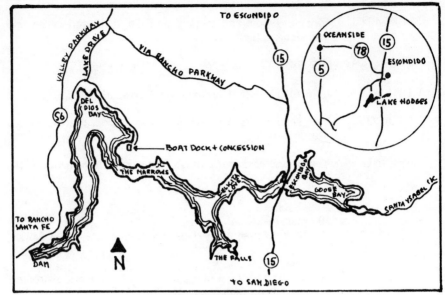

LAKE HODGES

Lake Drive, Del Dios (Escondido) CA 92025
Phone: (619) 668-2050

Elevation 330 feet   Surface Acres 1,234

Lake Hodges is located approximately 108 miles southeast of Los Angeles and 31 miles north of San Diego. From Los Angeles take Hwy 5 south to Oceanside, east on Hwy 78 to Hwy 15, south one mile on Hwy 15 to Valley Parkway, right on Valley Parkway, 3 miles to lake.

OPEN	Early March through late Fall, sunrise to sunset. Wednesdays, Saturdays, and Sundays.
FEES	State fishing license required. Adults, $4 per day; 8 to 15 years, $2, under 8, free.
BOAT RENTALS	Phone (619) 390-0222, Monday – Friday: 9 a.m. – 5 p.m. Boats held one hour after opening, day of reservation.
	Boat only $8 per day, $ 6 half day
	With motor 25 per day, 20 half day
BOAT LAUNCH	$5 per day. Paved launching ramp. No motor size limit, but maximum speed limit, 20 mph. Inflatable boats are OK, see Inflatable's Section. Canoes and kayaks, OK.
FISH & LIMITS	Bass – 5 (15" minimum size); channel cats – 5; crappie – 25; bluegill and bullheads – no limit.

FISH CLEANING	There are no cleaning facilities at present.
BAIT	Golden and red shiners (**no other minnows allowed**), water-dogs, mudsuckers, crawfish, crickets, worms, and lures OK.
SWIMMING	No.
WADERS	Yes. Tube fishing, OK.
PICNICKING	There is a small area, with tables and other facilities.
WATERSKI	No.
SAILING	Yes, including catamarans, no sinks or toilets.
WINDSURF	Yes.
HUNTING	No.
CAMPING	No. Nearest at Lake Dixon, (619) 741-3328.
STORES	Lake concession has food, drinks, bait, tackle, permits, and licenses. Other stores within 2 to 5 miles of the lake.
MOTELS	Many on Hwy 15 and in Escondido, 5 miles north.
GENERAL	Lake Hodges is under the jurisdiction of the City of San Diego Lakes Recreation Program, Water Utilities Department, 5540 Kiowa Drive, La Mesa, CA 91942; Phone (619) 668-2050.

This lake was closed for a number of years and was re-opened to the public in the Spring of 1977. There have been some nice fish caught since it's opening. The largest bass was 20 pounds, 4 ounces, and the channel cat record stands at 35 pounds, even.

Bluegill are nice size and lots of fun to catch. The crappie planted in 1978 have really started to produce. A 3 pound, 8 ounce was caught in 1987. The re-opening of Hodges has added to our much-needed lake recreation in Southern California.

Twenty-four hour fish report: (619) 465-FISH.

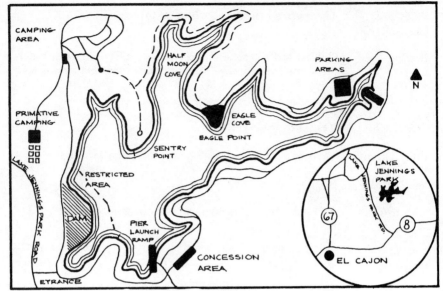

LAKE JENNINGS

9535 Harritt Road, Lakeside, CA 92040
Phone: (619) 443-2510

Elevation 700 feet   Surface Acres 178

Lake Jennings is approximately 20 miles northeast of San Diego. East from Hwy 5 and I-15 on Hwy 8 past El Cajon; 6 miles to Lake Jennings Park Road. Turn north (left) on Lake Jennings Park Road to lake entrance on the right.

OPEN & FEES	Year round, Fridays, Saturdays, & Sundays, with night fishing during the summer months. State fishing license required. Adults, $4.25 per day; seniors, $4.00; under 16 years, $2.50 per day; under 8, no charge with paid adult. Trout caught by children count on paid permit. Sightseeing 50¢ per person.
BOAT RENTALS	No reservations. First come, first served. Boat only $10 per day, $8 p.m. only With motor 20 per day; 15 p.m. only
BOAT LAUNCH	$3.00 per day. Minimum size 9', 2 man; paved ramp. Speed limit, 10 mph. Refundable $5.00 deposit required.
FISH & LIMITS	Large mouth bass, 5 (12" size limit); channel cats, 5; trout, 5; blue cats, 5; bullhead cats, 5; crappie, 25; red ear sunfish and bluegill, no limit. Fish cleaning in camping area on north side of lake for campers only.
BAIT	Golden & red shiners (no other minnows allowed), waterdogs, mudsuckers, crawfish, crickets, worms, & lures OK.

PICNICKING - SAILING - WATERSKI - SWIMMING - WADERS, TUBE FISHING - No.

FISHING FLOAT - Yes. 100-foot fishing float with handicapped access.

CAMPING   Reservations may be made 12 weeks in advance; three weeks by phone, and less than three weeks in person. Contact County of San Diego Parks and Recreation Department, 5201 Ruffin Road, Suite P, San Diego, CA 92123; Phone: (619) 565-3600.

Approximately 35 spaces for trailers and campers, with electricity, water, and sewer hook-ups, table and stove $16.00 per day.

Approximately 35 spaces for small campers and trailers with stove and tables, water and electricity, $14.00 per day.

Twenty developed tent spaces, water nearby, table, stove, and pantry. $10.00 per night.

STORES   Bait and limited supplies can be obtained at the concession store on Fridays, Saturdays, and Sundays. There are many stores within 1½ miles of lake.

MOTELS   There are many motels within a four-mile radius.

GENERAL   Lake Jennings is under the jurisdiction of the Helix Water District, 8111 University Avenue, La Mesa, CA 91944; Phone (619) 466-0585.

Campers may fish from the shore in the open area any day of the year with a permit from Ranger at the entrance station. Children under 16 must be accompanied by an adult. Children under 7 years will be admitted free when accompanied by a paying adult.

Pets in campground only; must be on leash no longer than 6'; no animals permitted below the diversion ditch level at any time. $1.00 per day per dog.

No hunting. No firearms, bows, arrows, or spears are allowed.

Trout are normally planted each week during fishing season. The largest caught so far was weighed in at 15 pounds; bass to 16 pounds, 5 ounces; blue cats to 46 pounds; red ear sunfish to 3 pounds, 1 ounce; and crappie to 2 pounds, 14 ounces are the largest of each species that have been caught to date. There are large bluegill that also add to the fun.

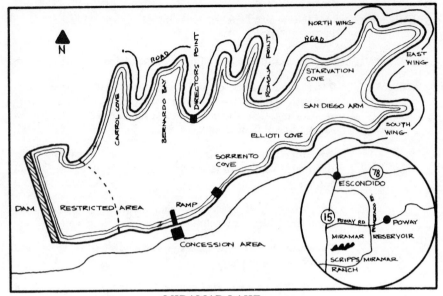

MIRAMAR LAKE
Miramar, CA 92145
Phone: (619) 668-2050

Elevation 714 feet   Surface Acres 162

Miramar Lake is located 114 miles southeast of Los Angeles and 18 miles north of San Diego. From Hwy 15 take Mira Mesa Blvd., east to Scripps Ranch Blvd., south to Scripps Lake Blvd., east to lake.

OPEN	Sunrise to sunset; early November to mid-October. Open Monday, Tuesday, Saturday, Sunday, and holidays, except New Year's, Christmas, and Thanksgiving.
FEES	State fishing license required. During trout planting season, fees are: Adults, $4.50 per day; 8 to 15 years, $2.50; age 7 and under, free. Otherwise permits are: Adults, $4.00 and $2.00 ages 8 to 15 years.
BOAT RENTALS	Reservations, (619) 390-0222, Monday – Friday; 9 a.m. to 5 p.m. Boats held half hour after sunrise the day of the reservation.

Boat only	$ 8.00 per day; $6.00 half day
With motor	25.00 per day; 20.00 half day

BOAT LAUNCH	$5.00 per day. Paved ramp. Speed limit, 5 mph; no maximum HP. Canoes and kayaks, OK; inflatables, OK. See section on Inflatables.

FISH & LIMITS	Florida bass, 5 (12" minimum size); trout, 5; channel cats, 5; bluegill and red ear sunfish - no limit.
BAIT	Golden and red shiners (**no other minnows allowed**), water-dogs, mudsuckers, crawfish, crickets, worms, and lures OK.

FISH CLEANING - None.

SWIMMING - WATERSKI - No.

WADERS	Yes. Tube fishing, OK.
PICNICKING	Yes. There are facilities for picnicking.
SAILING	Yes, including catamarans; no sinks or toilets.
CAMPING	No. Nearest is at Dixon Lake - See page 116.
STORES	The lake concession sells sandwiches, beverages, bait, tackle, permits, and licenses. Other stores are close by in Mira Mesa.
MOTELS	There are many up and down Highway 15.
GENERAL	Miramar Lake is under the jurisdiction of the City of San Diego Lakes Recreation Program, Water Utilities Department, 5540 Kiowa Drive, La Mesa, CA 91942; Phone (619) 668-2050.

Florida bass were planted in Miramar Lake, along with the other San Diego City Lakes, approximately 30 years ago. In 1971 the state record was broken with a 16 pound, 11 ounce catch. In 1973, this record was broken again with a catch of 20 pounds and 15 ounces.

The record on catfish stands at 21 pounds, 4 ounces.

Trout are planted weekly from November to June each year. Trout fishing is usually good at Miramar during this time. The largest one caught so far weighed in at 9 pounds, 7 ounces.

Twenty-four hour fish report: (619) 465-FISH.

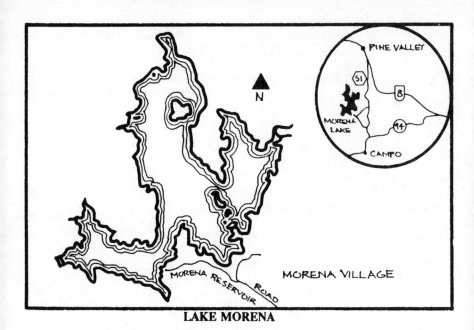

LAKE MORENA

San Diego County Parks and Recreation Department
5201 Ruffin Road, Suite P, San Diego, CA 92123
Phone: Lake (619) 478-5473 — Parks (619) 694-3049

Elevation 3,020 feet   Surface Acres, 1,500

Morena Lake is located approximately 60 miles east of San Diego. Take Hwy 8 east to Buckman Springs Road, turn south (right) on Buckman Springs Road approximately 9 miles to Lake Morena Road, turn right to the lake.

OPEN   The lake is open year round, half hour before sunrise to half hour after sunset.

FEES   Fishing fee, $3.50, 16 and older; $2.00 for 8 – 15 years; 7 and under, free. Disabled and age 62 and over, $2.00 weekdays, only. State fishing license required. Day use parking, $2.00.

BOAT   Boats only $8.00 per day; 6.00 1/2 day
RENTALS   With motor   25.00 per day; no 1/2 day
            Boat only, Senior/Disabled   4.00 per day; 3.00 1/2 day
            (weekdays)

BOAT   The launching ramp is paved. Launch fee, $4.00. Maximum
LAUNCH   size, 20'. No motor size limit, speed limit, 10 mph. INFLA-
            TABLES SAME AS SAN DIEGO CITY LAKES.

FISH & LIMITS	There are bass - 5 (12" size limit); channel cats - 10; trout - 5; crappie - 25; bluegill, bullheads, and red ear sunfish - no limit. Excellent enclosed fish cleaning building with stainless steel cleaning tables, lights, and water.
BAIT	Golden & red shiners (no other minnows allowed); waterdogs, mudsuckers, crawfish, crickets, worms, & lures OK.
SAILING	Yes. Small sailboats like Hobie Cats - $4.00 daily use fee for sailboats, $25.00 annual fee. Windsurfing, OK.

WADERS - TUBE FISHING - OK.

SWIMMING - HUNTING - WATERSKIING - JETSKIS - Not allowed.

CAMPING	Lake Morena Park is open every day, year round. Call (619) 565-3600 for reservations. Res. fee $3.00.
	There are 58 campsites with water and electricity for $12.00 per night. 28 developed campsites (no hook-ups) with water and showers and restroom, $10.00 per night. North Shore: Primitive campsites for RV and tents, $8.00 per night. Seniors and disabled, may purchase discount cards good the year round. Call for group and caravan rates.
	There is also a private campground, Lake Moreno RV Park (619) 478-5677 for travel trailers, campers, and motor homes, with complete hook-ups.
PETS	Pets are $1.00 per day, must be on 6' leash.
STORES	There are stores, restaurants, and gas stations within 1-5 miles of the park where you can buy bait, gas, licenses, propane, food, drinks, and supplies.
MOTORBIKES	Street legal and comply with park rules. Check with the Ranger. NO OFF ROADS.
GENERAL	Lake Morena is under the jurisdiction of the San Diego County Parks and Recreation Department, 5201 Ruffin Road, Suite "P", San Diego, CA 92123; Call (619) 694-3049.
	Lake Morena is located in the mountains 63 miles east of San Diego. This is very scenic country with large granite boulders and oak trees. Fishing for bluegill is fantastic. A stringer of these 3/4 pound scrappers is much fun and excellent eating. The record bluegill went to 2 pounds, 4 ounces. Bass over 19 pounds, 3 ounces are caught. Spring brings fine crappie fishing to 2 pounds. Record catfish was 16 pounds, 2 ounces. Trout, 9 pounds, 6 ounces.
	Even though it is 170 miles from Los Angeles, the dyed-in-the-wool fisherman will be glad to make the trip.

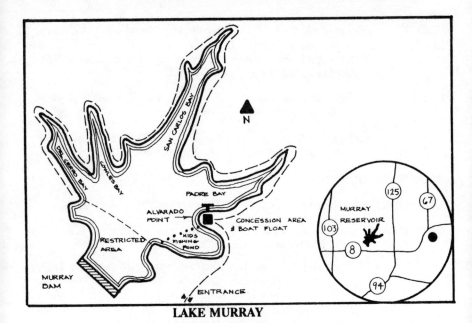

LAKE MURRAY

San Diego, CA 92101
Phone: (619) 668-2050

Elevation 541 feet   Surface Acres 198

Lake Murray is northeast of San Diego. Go east on Hwy 8 from Hwy 5 in Mission Valley to Lake Murray Blvd., north on Lake Murray Blvd., to Kiowa Drive, turn left to lake.

OPEN
Lake Murray will be open from sunrise to sunset for fishing, starting in November, through Labor Day; Open days will be Wednesdays, Saturdays, Sundays, and holidays, except New Year's, Thanksgiving, and Christmas. Lake Murray is open year round sunrise to sunset for walking, jogging, and picnicking.

FEES
State fishing license required. During **trout season** fees are: adults $4.50 per day; 8 - 15 years, $2.50; age 7 and under, free. Otherwise permits are: Adults, $4.00; ages 8 - 15 years, $2.00 per day.

BOAT RENTALS
Phone (619) 390-0222; Monday through Friday, 9 a.m. to 5 p.m. Boats held one hour after opening the day of reservations.

Boat only	$8.00 per day; $6.00 half day
With motor	25.00 per day; 20.00 half day

No private motors allowed on rentals.

BOAT LAUNCH - $5.00 per day - paved ramp. Speed limit, 10 mph.

FISH & LIMITS	Bass - 5 (12" size limit); trout - 5; channel cat - 5; crappie - 25; no limit on bluegill.
FISH CLEANING	There are no fish cleaning facilities at the lake.
BAIT	Golden and red shiners (**no other minnows allowed**). Water-dogs, mudsuckers, crawfish, crickets, worms, and lures OK.

WADERS - TUBE FISHING - No.

SWIMMING - SAILING - WATERSKI - HUNTING - No.

PICNICKING	Yes. Also excellent areas for hiking and walking.
CAMPING	Nearest camping at Lake Jennings, (619) 565-3600.
STORES	Food and beverages, permits, bait, tackle, and licenses can be purchased at the lake concession. There are many stores three miles from lake in La Mesa area.
MOTELS	There are many motels along Hwy 8 and in La Mesa area.
GENERAL	Lake Murray is under the jurisdiction of the San Diego Lakes and Recreation Department, Water Utilities Department, 5540 Kiowa Drive, La Mesa, CA 91942. Call (619) 668-2050.

Florida bass were introduced to Lake Murray over 20 years ago and have done well in most of the San Diego lakes. These bass grow twice as fast and much larger than the Northern Large Mouth. Many have been caught in the 10 to 15 pound bracket. The largest one caught in Lake Murray weighed 17 pounds, 14 ounces.

Catfish grow to whopper size here. The largest cat caught here was a lunker weighing 32 pounds, 11 ounces.

Twenty-four hour fish report: (619) 465-FISH.

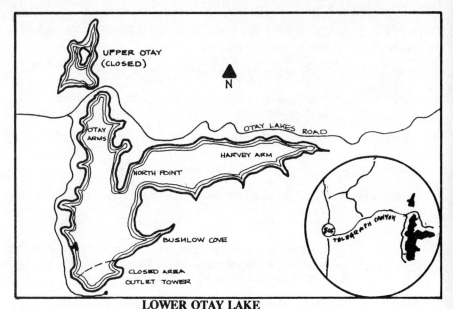

LOWER OTAY LAKE

Chula Vista, CA 92010
Phone: (619) 668-2050

Elevation 491   Surface acres 1,266

Lower Otay Lake is 20 miles southeast of San Diego and 8
miles east of Chula Vista. Go south through San Diego on
Hwy 805 to Telegraph Canyon Road, east on Telegraph
Canyon to Wueste Road, turn right to lake.

OPEN   Sunrise to sunset, mid-January through Fall on Wednesday,
Saturday, Sunday, and holidays; except Thanksgiving, Christmas, and New Year's.

FEES   State fishing license required. Adults, $4 per day; ages 8 – 15,
$2.00; age 7 and under, free.
Boat only $8.00 per day; $6.00 half day
With motor   25.00 per day; 20.00 half day

BOAT
LAUNCH $5.00 per day; speed limit, 20 mph; no maximum HP. Paved
ramp. Canoes and kayaks, OK. Inflatables, see page 178.

FISH &
LIMITS   Florida bass, 5 (12" minimum size); channel, blue, and white
cats, 5; crappie, 25; bullheads and bluegill, no limit.

FISH
CLEANING   There are no fish cleaning facilities.

BAIT   Golden and red shiners (no other minnows allowed), water-dogs, mudsuckers, crawfish, crickets, worms, and lures OK.

WADERS - TUBE FISHING - OK.

PICNICKING   Yes.

WATERSKI   No.

SAILING   Yes, including catamarans, no sinks or toilets.

HUNTING   Yes. Duck. Open middle of October to January; Wednesdays and Saturdays, call (619) 668-2050 for reservations and exact opening dates.

CAMPING   None.

MOTELS   Many in Chula Vista, 8 miles west of the lake.

GENERAL   Lower Otay Lake is under the jurisdiction of the City of San Diego Lakes Recreation Program, Water Utilities Department, 5540 Kiowa Drive, La Mesa, CA 91942; Phone: (619) 668-2050.

                Florida bass were introduced to Lower Otay approximately 30 years ago. Since that time, many bass of the "whopper" class have been caught. The largest to date was a giant of 18 pounds, 12 ounces.

                Catfish do well here. The channel cat record is 38 pounds, 7 ounces; blue cat, 82.10 pounds (state record 4/24/96). Bluegill grow quite large as well. The record bluegill was 3 pounds, 8 ounces. Man, that's some bluegill. State record - crappie to 3 pounds, 6 ounces. Nice!

                Twenty-four hour fish report: (619) 465-FISH.

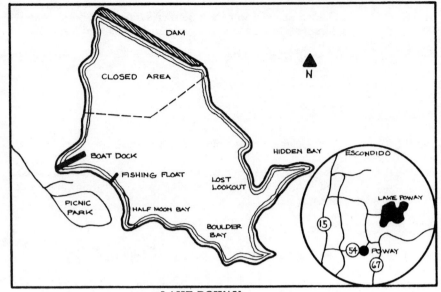

LAKE POWAY

14644 Lake Poway Road, Poway, CA 92074
Phones: (619) 679-5466
Concession: (619) 486-1234

Elevation 938 feet   Surface Acres 60

Lake Poway is 119 miles from Los Angeles and 26 miles from San Diego. From the Los Angeles area, go south on Hwy 5 to Oceanside. Turn east on Hwy 78 to I-15 in Escondido; go south on I-15 to Rancho Bernardo Road, turn east on Rancho Bernardo Road. This becomes Espola Road. Continue to Lake Poway Road, turn left to lake. Approximately 5 miles from I-15.

OPEN

Wednesday through Sunday, sunrise to sunset during the winter, sunrise to 11 p.m. during the summer. Closed Monday and Tuesday, Thanksgiving and Christmas.

FEES

Parking for day use, no charge for Poway residents. AUTO: April through October – weekends and holidays, $4.00. November to April – no charge. RVs and buses, $4.00; motorcycles, $1.00. No parking charge if fishing. Fishing fees: must have state fishing license. Lake permit, adult (16 and over) is $4.50; juniors (8-15 years) $2.00; under 8, free if fishing with an adult with permit.

BOAT
RENTALS

NO PRIVATE BOATS. Fifty boats available. No outboard motors allowed.

Boat only	$10.00 per day; $7.00 from noon on
With electric motor	15.00 per day; 12.00 from noon on

Only electric motors allowed. Five handicapped boats are available. Paddle boats, sailboats, and sabots for rent.

BOAT LAUNCH – No private boats, waders, or tube fishing.

FISH &
LIMITS

Florida and large mouth bass (12" size limit) in combo – 5; trout – 5; channel cats – 10; red ear sunfish – 25. Good fish cleaning facilities with boards, tables, and water.

BAIT

Golden & red shiners (**no other minnows allowed**), waterdogs, mudsuckers, crawfish, crickets, worms, & lures OK.

SWIMMING – WATERSKIING – WINDSURFING – No.

PICNICKING

Fifteen acres of rolling grass and shade trees with gazebos, braziers, fire rings, tables, Tot Lot, special use building, and a deep pit barbeque for special group use. Facilities for horseshoes, volleyball, and softball may be used.

CAMPING

Yes. There is an eight-site hike-in campground with running water and flush toilets.

STORES

A concession at the lake handles all kinds of bait, beer, tackle, deli-type food, and beverages. Phone: (619) 486-1234. There are many stores within 3 miles of the lake.

MOTELS

There are two in Poway; several in Rancho Bernardo and on Highway 15.

GENERAL

Lake Poway is a domestic water source fed by the Colorado River Aqueduct System. It is also a multi-purpose reservoir. Construction of the dam began in 1970; the dam and filtration plant were completed in late 1971, and the recreation facilities in September 1972. On November 4, 1972, the lake and park were opened for public use.

There are 50 miles of trails designed exclusively for hiking, nature walks, bicycling, and horseback riding; there is a fishing float lighted at night, for the convenience of shoreline and night fishermen.

32 thousand pounds of trout are stocked in the lake each year, October through May. 10,000 pounds of catfish are stocked during the summer months. Even though the lake has only been open since 1972, it has produced some very nice catches of fish. Bass to 17 pounds, 8 ounces, catfish to 28 pounds, 3 ounces; rainbow trout to 13 pounds, 2 ounces; red ear sunfish to 2 pounds. Fishing will get better and better as the present stock grows and multiplies.

The lake and park are under the jurisdiction of the City of Poway. Lake phone: (619) 679-5466.

Permit Office: Sells state licenses and permits, has boat rentals and information.

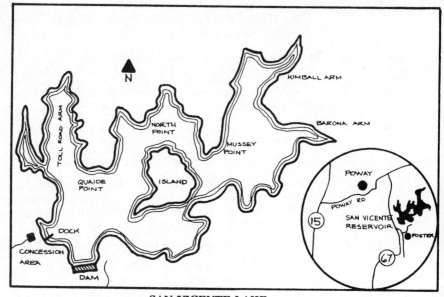

SAN VICENTE LAKE

Lakeside, CA 92040
Phone: (619) 668-2050

Elevation 659 feet   Surface Acres 1,069

San Vicente Lake is 123 miles southeast of Los Angeles. From Los Angeles go south on Hwy 5 past Oceanside to Hwy 78, east on Hwy 78 to I-15 in Escondido; south on I-15 to Rancho Bernard Road, east on to Hwy 67 south to Lake turn-off.

It is approximately 25 miles northeast of the City of San Diego; go east on Hwy 8 to Hwy 67 in El Cajon; north on Hwy 67 through Lakeside to Moreno Road, turn right one mile then left 1½ miles to the lake.

OPEN	For fishing – mid-October to Memorial Day; for waterskiing, from Memorial Day through September. Sunrise to sunset, Thursdays, Saturdays, Sundays, and holidays, EXCEPT Thanksgiving, Christmas, and New Year's.
FEES	State fishing license required. During trout season fees are: Adults, $4.50 per day; 8-15 years, $2.50; age 7 and under, free. Otherwise permits are: adults $4.00, ages 8-15 years, $2.00 per day. Waterski, $5.00, adults; $2.50 for juniors.
BOAT RENTALS	Reservations (619) 390-0222, Monday through Friday, 9 a.m. to 5 p.m. Reserved boat held half hour after opening.

Boat only $8.00 per day; $6.00 half day
With motor   25.00 per day; 20.00 half day

BOAT LAUNCH	$5.00 per day; paved ramp. Speed limit, 35 mph. No maximum HP. Canoes and kayaks, OK; inflatables, OK. See Section on Inflatables.
FISH & LIMITS	Bass - 5 (12" min. size); cats - 5; trout - 5; crappie - 25; bluegill and bullhead - no limit.
FISH CLEANING	There are no fish cleaning facilities at the lake, plans for the future.
BAIT	Golden and red shiners (no other minnows allowed); water-dogs, mudsuckers, crawfish, crickets, worms, and lures OK.
SWIMMING	No.

WADERS - TUBE FISHING - OK.

PICNICKING	Yes. Tables and facilities by the bait house. No fires allowed.
WATERSKI	Yes, from Memorial Day through September.
SAILING	Yes, mid-October through May only. Includes catamarans – minimum 10'; no toilets or sinks.
CAMPING	Nearest is Lake Jennings Campground (619) 565-3600.
STORES	Sandwiches, beverages, bait, tackle, licenses, and permits available at the lake concession. Many stores in Lakeside, 5 miles away.
GENERAL	San Vicente Lake is under the jurisdiction of the City of San Diego Lakes Recreation Program, Water Utilities Department, 5540 Kiowa Drive, La Mesa, CA 91942. Phone (619) 668-2050.

San Vicente Lake has always been a producer of large fish. The largest Florida bass weighed 18 pounds, 12 ounces. The largest blue cat was 57 pounds, 11 ounces; and channel cat to 27 pounds, 4 ounces.

Trout are planted each week from early November through May.

Bluegill and green sunfish are abundant but small; crappie are few, but large.

Twenty-four hour fish report: (619) 465-FISH.

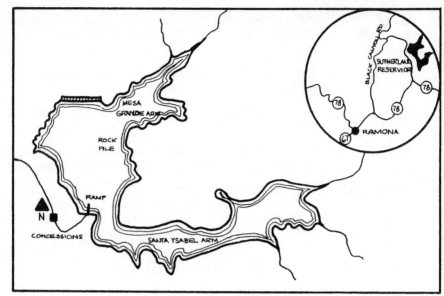

LAKE SUTHERLAND

22600 Sutherland Dam Road, Ramona, CA 92065
Phone: (619) 668-2050

Elevation 2,074 feet   Surface Acres 557 (Max)

Lake Sutherland is located approximately 138 miles southeast of Los Angeles and 45 miles northeast of San Diego. From Los Angeles, south on Hwy 5 to Oceanside (Carlsbad) turn east on Hwy 78 through Escondido, on to Ramona (35 miles). East on Hwy 78 six miles to Lake Sutherland turn-off, turn left for two miles to lake.

OPEN	Sunrise to sunset, March to late Fall. Open Friday, Saturday, Sunday, and holidays, except Thanksgiving, Christmas, and New Year's.
FEES	State fishing license required. Adults, $4.00 per day; 8-15 years, $2.00; age 7 and under, free.
BOAT RENTALS	Phone: (619) 390-0222. Monday – Friday, 9 a.m. to 5 p.m. Boats held half hour after sunrise, day of reservations.

BOAT
RENTALS

Boat only $8.00 per day; $6.00 half day
With motor   25.00 per day; 20.00 half day.

BOAT
LAUNCH

$5.00 per day. Paved ramp. Speed limit 20 mph. No maximum HP. Canoes and kayaks, OK. Inflatables, OK. See Section on Inflatables.

FISH & LIMITS	Florida bass (12" min. size), 5; channel and blue cats, 5; crappie, 25; bluegill, red ear sunfish, and bullheads, no limit. No fish cleaning facilities at the lake.
BAIT	Golden & red shiners (**no other minnows allowed**). Waterdogs, mudsuckers, crawfish, crickets, worms, & lures OK.

SWIMMING - WATERSKIING - No.

WADERS - TUBE FISHING - OK.

PICNICKING	Yes. Hiking also.
SAILING	Yes, includes catamarans; no sinks or toilets.
HUNTING	Waterfowl. Mid-October; January; Thursdays and Sundays only. For reservations and exact dates, call (619) 668-2050.
CAMPING	The nearest public campground is Dos Picos, which is located 5 miles west of the town of Ramona on Hwy 67 (12 miles west of Lake Sutherland). The address is: 17953 Dos Picos Park Road, just off Hwy 67.
	This is a San Diego County Campground. Call (619) 565-3600 for reservations.
	There are 56 sites with water and electricity for $14.00 per night. 41 can be reserved and 15 are on first come, first served basis. There are 12 tent sites at $10.00 per night. There is a dump station for self-contained vehicles.
STORES	Lake concession has food, drinks, bait, tackle, permits, and licenses. There are more stores in Ramona eight miles away.
MOTELS	There is one in Ramona, 8 miles southwest on Hwy 78.
GENERAL	Lake Sutherland is under the jurisdiction of the City of San Diego Lakes Recreation Program, Water Utilities Department, 5540 Kiowa Drive, La Mesa, CA 91942. Phone (619) 668-2050.
	The lake is nestled in a beautiful canyon with mountains on all sides. It is an excellent lake for bass, catfish, bluegill, and red ear sunfish. Bass have been caught up to 16 pounds, 2 ounces; cats to 43 pounds, 4 ounces; bluegill and red ear sunfish of the one-pound class and crappie to 3 pounds are not uncommon. So, if you are a fisherman, you will certainly enjoy this lake. If you just go along for the ride, you'll enjoy the beautiful Ramona Indian country scenery.
	Twenty-four hour fish report: (619) 465-FISH.

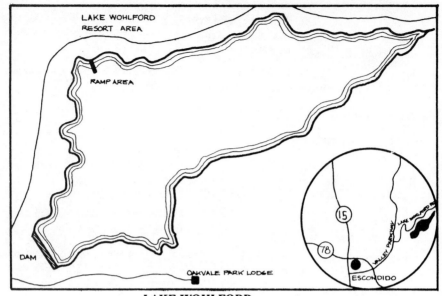

LAKE WOHLFORD

Escondido, CA 92025
Phone: Resort (619) 749-2755

Elevation 1,500 feet   Surface Acres 146

Lake Wohlford is 114 miles from Los Angeles and 41 miles from San Diego. Go east from Hwy 15 in Escondido on Valley Parkway, to Lake Wohlford turn-off; turn right 1½ miles to lake resort (see insert).

OPEN

Sunrise to sunset from December to September (check for exact dates) seven days per week.

FEES

State fishing license required. Adults, $4.50 per day (over 60, $3.50); 8-15 years, $2.50 per day; under age 7, free.

BOAT RENTALS

There are no boat reservations – all boats available on first come, first served basis. Rental rates are:
Boats only $8.00 per day; $6.00 half day
With 3 HP motor   18.00 per day; 14.00 half day

BOAT LAUNCH

Boat permit; $4 per day. Maximum 20'; minimum, 10'. Speed limit, 5 mph; paved ramp.

FISH & LIMITS

Bass – 5 (12" minimum size); trout, 5; channel cats, 5; crappie, 25; bluegill and bullheads, no limit.

FISH CLEANING

For those staying at Oakvale Park, there are excellent facilities in the campground.

BAIT	Golden and red shiners (**no other minnows allowed**). Water-dogs, mudsuckers, crawfish, crickets, worms, and lures OK.
SWIMMING	Not in lake; there is a pool at motel for guests. No waders or tube fishing.
CAMPING	There are two nice areas:

1. **Lake Wohlford Resort** (619) 749-2755 on north shore, 25484 Lake Wohlford Road, Escondido, CA 92027. Trailers – full hook-up, $12 per night for 4 persons plus 50¢ for each additional person. $70 per week for 4 persons; $2 per week for each additional person. $304 per month for mobile home units.

2. **Oakvale Park** (619) 749-2895 on south side of lake; 14900 Oakvale Road, #268, Escondido, CA 92027.

15 full hook-ups	$14.00 per day
41 electricity/water	12.00 per day
15 campsites	10.00 per day

MOTORBIKES	Street legal. On roads only. Not allowed in campgrounds.
STORES	Both Lake Wohlford Resort and Oakvale have stores with beer, wine, groceries, ice, motor fuel, bait, fishing licenses, and lake permits. Lake Wohlford Resort has a restaurant.
PICNICKING	There are a few tables next to the boat launch.
MOTELS	Lake Wohlford Resort has 10 units. All include housekeeping, $35.00 per night for 2 people Sunday to Thursday, holidays excluded; $2.16 extra for each additional person. Swimming pool for guests only. Many motels 6½ miles in Escondido.
AIRPORT	Airport is 1,500 to 1,700 feet by 100 feet wide. Has tie downs. Landing is by permission only.
GENERAL	Lake Wohlford is under the jurisdiction of the City of Escondido, Parks and Recreation Department, 201 North Broadway, Escondido, CA 92025.

This lake has been a fine fishing lake for many years. The facilities are very good, and the fishing can be from good to excellent. Trout are planted up to June 1st; the largest caught to date was 9 pounds, 14 ounces. Bass to 19-3/4 pounds. Crappie and bluegill fishing can be fantastic at times. The largest crappie was 4 pounds, 2 ounces, and bluegill was 2 pounds, 2 ounces. Cats to 28 pounds.

This is an excellent place to take the kids.

DOANE POND

Phone: (619) 742-3462

Elevation 5,500 feet   Surface Acres 3

This is a small pond located in Palomar State Park. Take Hwy 75 east from I-15 through Rincon. Turn left on S 6 to the top of the mountain to S 7; left on S 7 to Doane Pond.

Trout are planted periodically (limit 5). Must have state fishing license. No boats; only shore fishing, as this is a small three-acre pond.

Day use: $5.00. Dogs must be on a leash and kept in the developed areas (keep off trails); $1.00 per day or $1.00 over night for each dog.

Thirty-one family campsites. (Summer) $15.00 weeknights, $16.00 Friday and Saturday. (Winter) $12.00 per night. Flush toilets and hot showers. Reservations necessary, call MISTIX 1-800-444-7275.

Many trails for hiking in mountain meadows and through the pine trees.

There are 36 picnic sites with wood stoves; water and restrooms nearby.

A good place to rest and visit Palomar Observatory.

o o o o

GUAJOME LAKE

Now open; call (619) 694-3049 for information.

o o o o

HOLLINS LAKE

Now a Bird Sanctuary

o o o o

LOVELAND LAKE

Loveland will be opened after a land exchange between the Sweetwater authority and the Cleveland National Forest has been completed. The date is not definite, but it should be completed by early 1997. Loveland Lake is under the jurisdiction of the Sweetwater Authority, 505 Garrett Avenue, Chula Vista, CA 91910. Call (619) 420-1413 for opening information.

o o o o

O'NEILL LAKE

Closed to the Public

UPPER OTAY LAKE

Chula Vista, CA 92010
Phone: (619) 668-2050

Elevation 555 feet   Surface Acres approximately 80

Upper Otay is located a short distance above (north) of Lower Otay. Follow directions to Lower Otay. When you reach Wueste Road, go approximately 3/8 mile further east to Upper Otay gate on the north (left) side of road. Turn left to lake.

OPEN
Sunrise to sunset mid January through fall on Wednesdays, Saturdays, Sunday, and holidays; except Thanksgiving, Christmas, and New Year's.

FEES
State fishing license required – adults $4.00 per day, ages 8-15 $2.00, age 7 and under free. Pick up your fishing pass at Lower Otay concession.

BOATS
No boat rentals – no private boats – waders and tube fishing OK.

FISH & LIMITS
Bass – catch and release only with barbless hooks; bluegill and bullheads – no limit. No fish cleaning facilities.

BAIT
Bass – artificial lures with barbless hooks only. Red and meal worms OK for bluegill and bullheads.

PICNICKING
Yes for permit holders – plenty of room. Very few facilities – portable rest rooms.

WATERSKI – JETSKI – SAILING – WINDSAIL – CAMPING – No.

HUNTING
Yes, mid-October through mid-January Wednesdays and Saturdays until noon.

MOTELS
Many 10-15 miles from lake.

GENERAL
Upper Otay is under the jurisdiction of the city of San Diego Water Utilities Department, 5540 Kiowa Drive, La Mesa, CA, phone: (619) 668-2050.

o o o o

SAN DIEGUITO LAKE

Closed to the Public

o o o o

SANTEE LAKES

Santee Lakes Regional Park and Campground
P. O. Box 719003, Santee, CA 92072
Phone: (619) 448-2482

Elevation 369 feet   Seven Lakes; Surface Acres 7 to 13

Santee Lakes are located 17 miles east of San Diego. Go out Mission Gorge Road, north on Carlton Hills Blvd., to Carlton Oaks Drive, left to entrance.

Open year round; 8 a.m. to 7 p.m. May through October daily. From 8 a.m to sunset in winter.

Row boats are rented at $5.00 per hour. No fishing from row boats – bank fishing only. No tube fishing. No private boats.

State fishing license required.

Vehicles, $3.00 per day, Saturday, Sunday, and holidays. $2.00 Monday through Friday; fishing permits; adults, $4.00 per day; Ages 7-15 years, $2.00.

Camping year round. Reservations, call (619) 448-2482. 152 full hook-ups at $20.00 per night. The campground has restrooms, showers, swimming pool, propane station, laundromat, and game room. Weekly and monthly rates available.

There is a general store where you can buy groceries and supplies. Many stores and motels nearby.

There are bass to 10 pounds, 15 ounces; bluegill to 1-3/4 pounds, blue cats to 46 pounds and red ear sunfish over 1 pound, with limits of bass (12" minimum size), 5; channel cats, 5; trout, 5; bluegill and red ear, 20 each. All baits OK, except minnows.

There are fish cleaning facilities at the lake.

There is picnicking at the park.

A good place to take the family.

o o o o

SWEETWATER LAKE

Closed to the Public

o o o o

WINDMILL LAKE

Closed to the Public

Smith at Hodges with 9-pound Lunker.

**Mike Lum with 11 pound
Hodges lunker**

Randy Best with Southerland blade fish

Mark with his first 6 pounder.

Dennis K with
El Capitan 5 pounder

Dean R. with 6 pound
San Vicente catch -151-

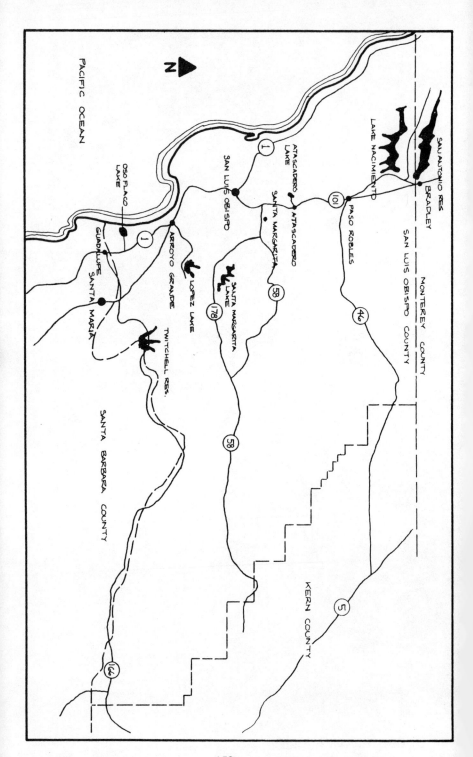

ATASCADERO LAKE

Highway 41, Atascadero, CA 93422
Phone: Park Supervisor (805) 461-5000

Elevation 834 feet   Surface Acres 30

This is a small lake located approximately 224 miles northwest of Los Angeles. Take Hwy 101 to Atascadero (16 miles past San Luis Obispo), turn left on Hwy 41, (west) one mile to lake.

OPEN

Year round; 6 a.m. to 10 p.m. day use only.

FEES

State fishing license is required, but there is no fishing fee.

BOAT RENTAL

Rental boats to paddle - but none for fishing.

BOAT LAUNCH

There is a boat launch for private boats (not paved) and there is no launching fee. No gas powered boats; no minimum size; must be safe; one life saving device per person.

FISH & LIMITS

They have bass - limit 5 (12" size limit); trout - 5; catfish - 20; crappie - 25; bluegill - no limit. No fish cleaning.

BAIT

No minnows brought in.

PICNICKING

Yes, throughout the park with permanent barbeques and playgrounds.

TUBE FISHING/WADERS - Yes.

WATERSKI - CAMPING - SWIMMING - No.

SAILING

Yes. Small craft only.

STORES

Within one to two miles, where you can buy anything.

MOTELS

One mile in Atascadero.

GENERAL

This small lake is under the jurisdiction of Atascadero Parks and Recreation Department, 6500 Palma, Atascadero, CA 93422; (805) 461-5000. Local park staff (805) 461-5085.

Even though this is a small lake, it has produced some fine fish. Bass to 9 pounds, cats to 15 pounds, crappie to 3½ pounds, and bluegill over a pound.

In addition to fishing, picnicking, kiddie pool, etc., there is a zoo that is open to the public. So, take the kids and have a fine trip. $2.50 adults; 3 to 17 years, $1.00; under 2 years, free. Seniors, $1.25.

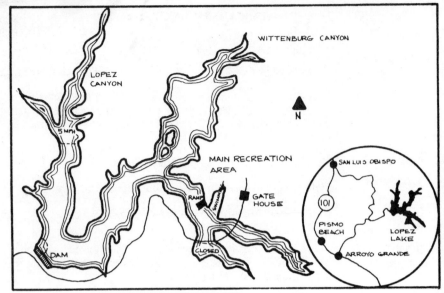

LOPEZ LAKE

6800 Lopez Drive, Arroyo Grande, CA 93420
Phone: Gate (805) 489-1122; (805) 489-8019

Elevation 520 feet   Surface Acres 974

Lopez Lake is located approximately 190 miles northwest of
Los Angeles. From Los Angeles take Hwy 101 north to the
town of Arroyo Grande. Take Grand Avenue off-ramp, north.
Follow signs along Lopez Drive, seven miles to lake.

OPEN	Year round. 7 days per week. Fishing; State Fishing Game Regulations. Half hour before sunrise to half hour after sundown. Twenty-four hours to camping.
FEES	No fishing fees. State fishing license required. Motor vehicle pass; $5.00 per day; $50 annual; Seniors $45.00; animals $1.50 per day. Must be licensed and have rabies shots.

BOAT
RENTALS   Reservations: (805) 489-1006. Also, pontoon boats, canoes, and
ski boats:

Boat only/4 pass	$30.00 per day;	$15.00 half day
Boat only/6 pass	30.00 per day;	15.00 half day
With motor/4 pass	45.00 per day;	35.00 half day
With motor/6 pass	45.00 per day;	35.00 half day

BOAT
LAUNCH   Paved ramp. Min. size, 8'; speed limit, 40 mph. Boat permits,
$4.00 per day; $50.00 per year; Seniors, $45.00; slips, $7.00 per
day; $30.00 per week; slips $65.00 per month; $650 per year.
You can shore-tie overnight in designated areas, if camping.

FISH & LIMITS	Bass, 5 (min. size 12"); catfish, 20; trout, 5; crappie, 25; red ear sunfish, green perch, bluegill, no limit. There are two fish cleaning stations in the area.
BAIT	No live bait allowed, only worms and lures.
SWIMMING	Yes, in designated areas. Waders and tube fishing OK.
PICNICKING	Over 200 acres for camping and picnicking, with tables, barbeque pits, and water; many hiking trails.

WATERSKI - WINDSURF - Yes. In designated areas. Sunup to sundown.

CAMPING	Over 200 acres with 350 sites. Reservations may be made by calling (805) 489-8019; 8 a.m. to 5 p.m. Monday through Friday. VISA and MASTERCARD accepted.

FAMILY CAMPSITES (in addition to vehicle pass fee):

Regular campsite	$13.00 per unit per day
With electricity	15.00 per unit per day
Full hook-up (sewer, wtr, elec)	20.00 per unit per day
Each extra vehicle	5.00 per unit per day

Camping limit is 15 calendar days in any 30-day period during the season April through September 30. Group reservations may be made by phone (805) 489-8019, or by letter; County General Services Department, Government Building, San Luis Obispo, CA 93408.

STORES	Yes. In the village next to the boat launch you can buy licenses, groceries, food, drinks, camping supplies, gas, boat repairs, bait, and tackle. Many others in town, 12 miles from the lake.
MOTELS	Many along Hwy 101, 12 miles from lake.
MOTORBIKES	Street legal. Approved muffler, Ridden only on the blacktop roads or other designated areas between the hours of 8 a.m. to 8 p.m. Mopeds, same.
GENERAL	Lopez Lake is under the jurisdiction of General Services Department of San Luis Obispo County. Phone (805) 781-5930. It is located at the Lopez Lake Recreation Area which covers an area of 4,300 acres. The area now covered by the lake was once a very active site where Chumash Indians hunted game and ground acorns into meal that was used as a cooked mush or made into flat bread. The area still contains reminders of the early Indian settlements.

Lopez Lake has matured as a fishing lake since its opening in 1970. Trout to 10 pounds, 12 ounces; bass to 10 pounds, 1 ounce; crappie 3 pounds, 5 ounces; catfish to 40 pounds; and a record 4-pound red eared sunfish was caught in 1987. If you really give it a try, you'll get your share.

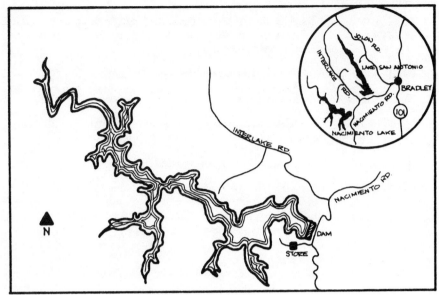

LAKE NACIMIENTO

Star Route, Box 2770, Bradley, CA 93426
Phone: (805) 238-3256 – 1-800-323-3839

Elevation 800 feet   Surface Acres 5,370

Lake Nacimiento is located approximately 241 miles northwest of Los Angeles. Take Hwy 101 to Paso Robles. Turn left (west) on Nacimiento Drive (24th Street), 16 miles to the lake. You can take Hwy 5 past Bakersfield to Hwy 46, turn left (west) to Paso Robles (63 miles).

OPEN & FEES
Open 24 hours per day, year round. Night fishing permitted. State fishing license required. $10 per day vehicle charge. $100 per year; $20 if you stay overnight. No fishing fee.

BOAT RENTALS
Reservations: (805) 238-1056 for all boats.
With motors   from $55 per day; $35 1/2 day
Bass, pontoon, ski, paddle boats, and canoes for rent.

SLIP
$10.00 per day; $50.00 per week; $150 per month. Dry storage available.

BOAT LAUNCH
Good paved launching facilities. $5.00 per day boat permit; annual permit, $55, good for Lake San Antonio as well as Nacimiento. Posted speed limit.

TRAILER RENTALS
Phone 1-800-323-3839. Camping trailers $95 per night.

FISH & LIMITS	Large mouth bass (12" min. size) and small mount bass (12" min. size) limit 5 in combination; five kinds of catfish, limit 20 in any combination; crappie, 25; white bass, bluegill, perch, and bullheads, no limit. Cleaning tables available.
BAIT	Mudsuckers, waterdogs, minnows OK. EXCEPT: No carp minnows allowed.
SWIMMING	There is swimming in the lake; also, a public pool and hot tubs. Waders and tube fishing OK.
PICNICKING	Yes. Many places to picnic.

WATERSKI - JETSKI - SAILING - WINDSURF - Yes.

HORSEBACK RIDING - HUNTING - None.

CAMPING	Yes. trailer, RVs, and tents. Two camps with 150 campsites $20 per night; $120 per week. No hookups. 40 sites full hook-up, $25; $150 per week. Restrooms and hot showers available. Winter rates available October 1 to March 1. Write or call for details: 1-800-323-3839. Senior and family rates available.
	Lodge rentals - call 1-800-323-3839 for reservations and information. Can accommodate up to 14 people. No pets allowed.
PETS	$3.00 per dog, per night. Owner must have current immunization tags in possession. Dog must be leashed.
MOTORBIKES	No motorbikes, mopeds, or motorcycles allowed in the resort area at any time.
STORES	You can get all kinds of supplies at the resort; food, drinks, camping supplies, bait, tackle, gas, ice, and licenses, etc. There is also a restaurant.
MOTELS	Many motels in Paso Robles, 16 miles away on Hwy 101.
GENERAL	Although Lake Nacimiento is in San Luis Obispo County, it is under the jurisdiction of Monterey County Parks Department, P. O. Box 367, Salinas, CA 93902; Phone: (408) 755-4895.
	Lake Nacimiento has approximately 165 miles of shore line, so it provides plenty of space for the fisherman to stretch out. It produces dandy catches of all varieties of fish. White bass were introduced in the lake in 1965 and replanted three times since. These bass have now established themselves and are providing excellent fishing. They will grow to 4 to 5 pounds.
	This is certainly a fine place to take the family, with excellent facilities and plenty of room.

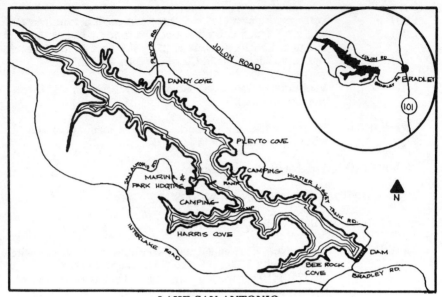

LAKE SAN ANTONIO

Bradley, CA 93426
Phone: Gate (805) 472-2311 — Fishing Report 1-800-310-2313
Stores and Information (805) 472-2313

Elevation 774 feet   Surface Acres 5,687

Lake San Antonio is located approximately 250 miles northwest of Los Angeles. Take Hwy 101 north to Paso Robles.
Turn left (west) on G 14 to lake. An alternate route: take Hwy
5 north past Bakersfield to Hwy 46, turn left (west) and follow
to Paso Robles, straight through on G 14 to lake.

OPEN   All year, 24 hours per day. Night fishing permit available.

FEES   State license required. No fishing fee. Auto permit, $6.00 per
              day, $55 per year. Shore fishing permitted.

BOAT   Reservations (805) 472-2818
RENTALS   With 10 HP $55.00 per day; $35.00 1/2 day
              Pontoon, ski, paddle, kayaks, and jetski rentals available.

BOAT   There are four 6-lane, paved launching ramps two on south
LAUNCH   side, two on north side, with 800,000 sq. ft. of surface parking
              area. Boats must meet state requirements. Boat, daily permit,
              $5.00; $55.00 annual. This is good for Nacimiento as well as
              San Antonio. Speed limit posted.

WET MOORING	$7.50 per day; $40.00 per week; $120.00 monthly; $450.00 yearly. Dry storage available.
FISH & LIMITS	Large mouth and small mouth bass (12" size limit), 5 in combination; catfish, 20 in combination; striped bass, limit 10 (no minimum size); crappie, 25; bluegill and red ear sunfish (perch), no limit. FISH CLEANING at each ramp.
BAIT	Waterdogs, mudsuckers OK. No carp minnows. Worms and lures OK.
SWIMMING	Yes. Nice sandy beaches. Lifeguard during summer months. Wader and tube fishing OK.
PICNICKING	Yes. Many areas to picnic, and trails to hike. $1.00 for dogs, limit two dogs.

WATERSKI - JETSKI - Yes. Areas marked, excellent for water skiing.

SAILING/WINDSURF - Yes. Boats checked by Monterey Co. Rangers.

MOTORBIKES Street legal. On road only. Licensed driver.

HORSEBACK RIDING - No. HUNTING - No.

CAMPING	643 regular sites on southside, and with overflow would total 2,000; 380 regular sites on northside and with overflow would total 400. Regular campsites $15.00 per night, summer; $13.00 per night, winter. Trailer type with utility hook-up, $19, summer; $17, winter. No charge for auto when camping. Seniors, $2.00 off all camping weekdays. Full hook-ups, $21.00, summer; $19, winter. (408) 755-4899.
STORES	Both sides have stores where you can buy bait, licenses, gas, ice, food, drink, and general supplies; others in Bradley and Paso Robles.
MOTELS	Lake San Antonio Resort at the lake has nice cabin rentals from $90 to $125 per night, summer; and $65 to $95 per night, winter. Call 1-800-310-2313 for reservations and information. There are motels on Hwy 101 or 30 miles in Paso Robles.
GENERAL	Although Lake San Antonio is in Monterey County and under the jurisdiction of the Monterey County Parks Department, P. O. Box 5249, Salinas, CA 93915; Phone: (408) 755-4895, it is a sister lake of Nacimiento Lake so included here.

This is a very large lake, with 65 miles of shore line. Fishing here can be from good to fantastic. There is a great variety of fish in the lake, so it provides for some interesting catches.

Since an annual boat permit is good at both San Antonio and Nacimiento, you can move back and forth over the 15 miles and try both lakes.

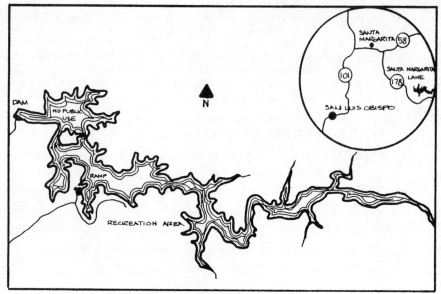

SANTA MARGARITA LAKE

Star Route Box 34, Santa Margarita, CA 93465
Phone: Gate (805) 438-5485

Elevation 1,301   Surface Acres 1,068

Santa Margarita Lake is located approximately 218 miles
northwest of Los Angeles. From Los Angeles go north on Hwy
101, eight miles past San Luis Obispo, turn right 2 miles to
Santa Margarita, then southeast, 8 miles on Pozo Road, to
lake entrance. Left at lake.

OPEN &
FEES
Year round, sunrise to sunset, 7 days per week. State fishing
license is required. No fishing fee. Auto permit, $5 per day;
$50 per year; $45.00 for Seniors. Animals, $1.50.

BOAT
RENTALS
(805) 438-3886.

Boat only	$35 per day; $25 half day
Summer w/6 HP motor	57 per day; 37 half day
Winter w/6 HP motor	55 per day; 35 half day
Summer w/9.9 HP motor	67 per day; 47 half day
Winter w/9.9 HP motor	65 per day; 45 half day

Slips $8.00 per day, $49 per month. Pontoon boats and kayak
rentals.

BOAT
LAUNCH
There are two excellent paved ramps for launching, $4.00 per
day; annual permit, $50; Seniors $45.00. Boat size minimum 8'
with 42" width. No maximum. Speed limit: posted from 5 mph
to 30 mph limit. $25 per month shore tie.

FISH & LIMITS	Black bass (12" size limit) - 5; striped bass - 10; catfish - 20; trout - 5; crappie - 25; bluegill and bullhead cats, no limit.
FISH CLEANING	There are excellent fish cleaning facilities located near the boat ramps.
BAIT	Lake rules do not permit any live bait. No minnows, mudsuckers, waterdogs. Only crawfish caught in the lake, crickets, worms, and lures are to be used.
SWIMMING	There is a swimming pool open during summer months. Day use and camping fee includes swimming. NO BODY CONTACT OR SWIMMING IN THE LAKE.
PICNICKING	Yes. At various spots along the lake. There are areas for picnicking, hiking, walking. Pets may be brought if kept on leash not exceeding six feet.
WATERSKI	No. No waders. Tube fishing is permitted.
SAILING	Yes, sailing is allowed. No restrictions on size of boat. Must be safe. No sail boards or rafts. Canoes and kayaks OK.
CAMPING	There is group camping inside the lake area. For reservations call (805) 489-8019. There are 46 individual campsites (no hook-ups), including boat in-sites at $13.00 per night. There is a dump station.

CAMPING (continued):

There are two private camp and trailer parks near the entrance:

Rinconada Trailer Park - (805) 438-5479.
4995 Santa Margarita Lake Road, Santa Margarita, CA 93453

$18 per day with complete hook-ups; 4 people $12 per day for camping in tents and self-contained vehicles; $15 with electricity. Hot showers and laundry. This park is 3/4 mile from the lake on Santa Margarita Lake Road.

Santa Margarita Lake KOA Campground - (805) 438-5618
4765 Santa Margarita Lake Road, Santa Margarita, CA 93453

$20 per night for two; $4 each additional person over 18 years, $3.00 under 18. Electrical hook up, $2.00; water plus $2.00; full hook-up, $6.00 additional. Pool, playground, hiking, groceries, dump station, and laundry facilities. Horse, hotel, and camping cabinets available. Winter rates vary.

STORES	Marina Store (805) 438-3886 has gas, ice, license, bait, and supplies. There is a store outside the gate near the highway. Others in Santa Margarita, 8 miles west.
MOTELS	There are numerous motels in San Luis Obispo & Atascadero.

GENERAL   The Santa Margarita Lake Recreational Area is operated by
the County of San Luis Obispo under its Department of
General Services; phone (805) 781-5200. 1035 Palm Street, San
Luis Obispo, CA 93408. This is a domestic water supply
reservoir formed by the Salinas Dam backing up the Salinas
River.

Santa Margarita Lake does not get the heavy fishing pressure
that other lakes get, possibly because of the distance from the
heavy population centers. This does not take away from the
fact that it is an excellent fishing lake. Bass, 10 pounds, 12
ounces; crappie, 3 pounds, 10 ounces; white cats, 12 pounds,
13 ounces; striped bass to 29½ pounds; channel cats to 24
pounds. Trout to 7½ pounds.

There are no firearms allowed, as all wild life is protected
within the recreational area.

o o o o

LAGUNA LAKE

Madonna Road, San Luis Obispo, CA 93401
Phone: Parks Department (805) 781-7300

Elevation 205 feet   Surface Acres Approx. 40

Laguna Lake is a small city lake located in a 400-acre park
(marsh) and wild life preserve approximately 208 miles
northwest of Los Angeles. Take Hwy 101 north to the Madonna off-ramp in the city of San Luis Obispo; go left 3/4 mile
on Madonna Road to lake entrance.

OPEN   Year round, sunup to sundown.

FEES   No fees of any kind, just state fishing license.

BOAT   There is a paved launching ramp (free launch). There is no
minimum or maximum on the size of boat, but this is a small
lake. No gasoline motors allowed. Electric motors only. There
are no boat rentals.

FISH &   There are bass (12" min. size) - limit 5; trout in season - 5;
LIMITS   catfish - 20; crappie - 25; bluegill - no limit.

FISH CLEANING - There are no fish cleaning facilities at lake.

BAIT   See California Sport Fishing Regulation for live bait permitted.

SWIMMING   This is discouraged as much of this is marsh land. Waders and
tube fishing OK.

PICNICKING Yes. There are tables, barbeques, and restrooms provided on
the grounds. Ground areas may be reserved - (805) 781-7300.

| SAILING | Yes. And also WINDSURFING. Since this is a small lake, it limits the size of boat you can sail comfortably. |

WATERSKI - CAMPING - None.

STORES	All the stores you want within three miles of the lake in San Luis Obispo.
MOTELS	Many up and down Hwy 101 and in the town of San Luis Obispo.
GENERAL	This small lake is under the jurisdiction of the San Luis Obispo City Parks and Recreational Department, 860 Pacific Street, San Luis Obispo, CA 93401; Phone: (805) 781-7300.

○ ○ ○ ○

OSO FLACO LAKE

Phone (805) 545-9925

Elevation, just about sea level   Surface Acres 110

Oso Flaco Lake is located approximately 190 miles northwest of Los Angeles. Take Hwy 101 north to Santa Maria. Turn west on Hwy 166, go 8 miles to Guadalupe. Turn north on Hwy 1, three miles to Oso Flaco Road. Turn west (left), go 3 miles to lake.

The area consists of two small lakes. The lake is open sunrise to sunset daily, year round. $2.00 daily fee for one person and auto. $4.00 for two or more people and auto.

A new foot bridge has just been built over the lake connecting with the beach boardwalk. A fun place for hikers and bird watchers.

A state fishing license is required. The only fish of importance in the lake is the large mouth bass. State limit is 5 (12" size limit). There is no boat ramp, so only small prams or car toppers could be launched - mostly carry-in boats. No motors.

There are no facilities for cleaning fish, buying food or bait. There are primitive restrooms in the parking area.

No swimming in the lake. No fires. Be sure to clean up your litter. Oso Flaco is a place to relax and enjoy nature.

Oso Flaco Lake is jointly managed by the Off Road Vehicle Division, California Department of Parks and Recreation and the Nature Conservancy - Phone (805) 545-9925. Mailing Address: P. O. Box 15810, San Luis Obispo, CA 93406.

WHALE ROCK RESERVOIR

108 Old Creek Road, Cayucos, CA 93430
Phone: (805) 995-3701

Elevation 50 feet   Surface Acres 580

Whale Rock Reservoir is located 226 miles northwest of Los Angeles. From Los Angeles take Hwy 101 (Ventura Fwy) west through Ventura and Santa Barbara to San Luis Obispo. Turn left (north) on Hwy 1, then 18 miles to Old Creek Road. Right on Old Creek Road to the lake.

Open season for Whale Rock is from the last Saturday in April through November 15th. State license required. Whale Rock is open Wednesday through Sunday and all holidays, 6 a.m. to 5 p.m., from the last Saturday in April through September 30; 8 a.m. to 5 p.m. from October 1 through November 15. Only 200 visitors are admitted at any one time on a first come, first served basis.

Admission fee is $2.00 per day for 16 years and older; $1.00 for 15 years and younger.

There are no boats for rent and no boats are allowed, just bank fishing in designated areas.

There are trout (limit 5) and suckers in the lake. If you catch suckers, management requests that you don't throw them back but keep them or put them in the garbage can. This will help rid the lake of the unwanted fish.

No live minnows allowed; mudsuckers, crawfish, crickets, worms, and lures OK.

There is no swimming, wading, or washing in the reservoir; in fact, no body contact, as this is a drinking water lake.

There is no camping.

Restrooms are provided throughout the fishing and parking lot areas. Please stay within the designated area (Johnson Cove to past Dead Horse Point).

Picnicking permitted, with tables provided. No open fires are allowed anywhere.

No guns allowed. Dogs must be on a leash.

There are no stores at the lake, so bring what bait, food, and drinks you need.

There are stores and motels, three miles in Cayucos.

Whale Rock Reservoir is under the jurisdiction of the City of San Luis Obispo, Utilities Department, 955 Morro Street, San Luis Obispo, CA 93401. Phone (805) 781-7215.

So, if it's "just a stroll around, bank fishing day" you want, give Whale Rock a try.

**Margaret W. with a
nice Lopez stringer**

Scott with a nice 6-pound 12-ounce Lopez bass.

**Bob G., Terry S., Al Yee, Terry B. and Scott with
8 Lopez bass to 7 pounds 2 ounces.**

Another Lopez camper.

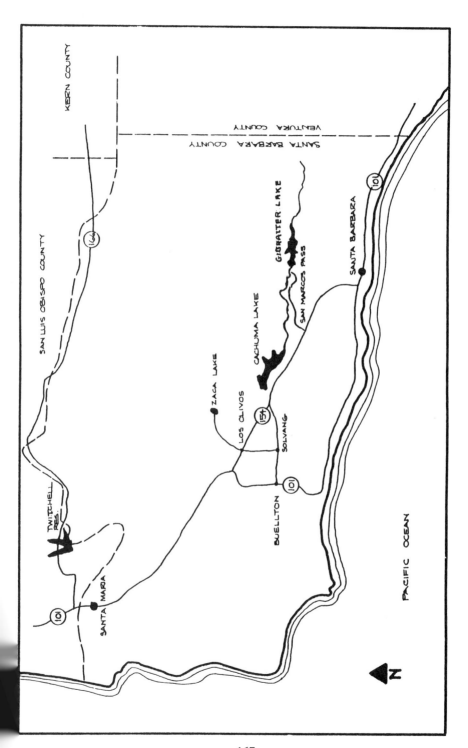

-167-

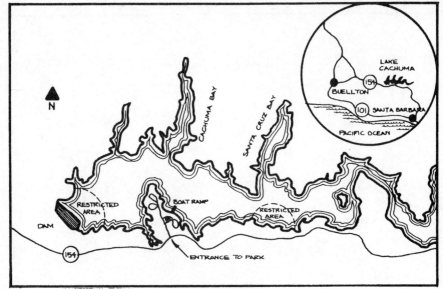

LAKE CACHUMA

Star Route, Santa Barbara, CA 93105
Phones: Gate House (805) 688-4658
Tackle Shop (805) 688-4040
Fish Report (213) 284-7908; (805) 688-7724

Elevation 650 feet   Surface Acres, 3,100

Lake Cachuma is located approximately 116 miles northwest
of Los Angeles. Take Hwy 101 north through Santa Barbara
to the San Marcos Pass turnoff. Take Hwy 154 over San
Marcos Pass, 24 miles to lake.

**OPEN &
FEES**
The lake is open the year round. Day use, 6 a.m. to 10 p.m.
Camping, 24 hours. State fishing license required. Autos, $5.00
per day; $40.00 per year (age 62, $30.00 per year).

**BOAT
RENTALS**
Reservations taken on full-day boats only: must incl. deposit.
Boat will be held all day. Write: Cachuma Boat Rentals, P.O.
Box 287, Solvang, CA 93464. Phone: (805) 688-4040.

Boat only, 4 pass.	$22 per day; $20 per 5 hours
Boat only, 6 pass.	32 per day; 26 per 5 hours

No motor over 10 HP allowed on rental boats.

5 HP, 4 pass.	$48 per day; $41 per 5 hours
5 HP, 6 pass.	58 per day; 50 per 5 hours
8 HP, 4 pass.	60 per day; 49 per 5 hours
8 HP, 6 pass.	72 per day; 57 per 5 hours
9.9 HP, 4 pass.	70 per day; 56 per 5 hours
9.9 HP, 6 pass.	82 per day; 64 per 5 hours

| BOAT LAUNCH | Annual permit, $40.00; age 62, $35.00; daily permit, $4.00. There is an paved launching ramp with adequate trailer parking. Minimum size boat allowable is 10' with at least 42" width and 12" depth. No boats that have toilet facilities or sink drains are allowed. Inflatables, see Page 178. No canoes, catamarans, kayaks, or rafts. |

MOORING ADVANCE RATES:

	Night	Week	Month	Year
Under 17 feet	$8	$35	$60	$600
17 to 20 feet	8.50	38	67	670
20 to 24 feet	9	41	77	770

Over 24 feet – by arrangement.

Speed limits; 5 mph in coves; 30 mph in center lane; 10 mph elsewhere.

| FISH & LIMITS | Large mouth and small mouth bass (min. size 12") --5 in combination; trout – 5; cats – 10; crappie – 25; red ear sunfish, bluegill no limit. There are two excellent fish cleaning facilities with boards, water, and lights. |

| BAIT | No minnows, mudsuckers, or waterdogs brought in. Shad in lake, OK. Crawfish, worms, and lures, OK. |

| SWIMMING | Body contact with water is not allowed in lake. However, there are swimming pools located east of the entrance gate. |

| PICNICKING | Yes. Day use only. Sites with tables and barbeque grills under the beautiful large oak trees. |

| WATERSKI | No. No waders. No tube fishing. |

| SAILING | Yes. Minimum boat 10' with 42" beam and 12" depth. |

HORSEBACK RIDING – There are no rentals as of 1995.

| GOLF | Not in park. Several championship courses nearby in Santa Barbara and Solvang. |

| PETS | $1.00 per day per dog; must be kept on leash, not allowed in boat. |

| MOTORBIKES | $5.00 per day permit. Bike must be "street legal". Operator must have a valid driver's license; operate on paved roads only. |

| CAMPING | Over 500 campsites are available for either tents or trailer camping; first come, first served. A fireplace and table are furnished with each campsite. Water and restrooms with hot showers, located nearby. Limit, April through September – 2 weeks stay in 30-day period; October through March – 60-day stay OK. No hook-ups. $13 per night; $78 per week per |

vehicle. Seniors $11 per night; $66 per week. Hook-ups – water, electric, and sewer, $18 per night; $108 per week. Seniors and handicapped, $15 per night; $90 per week per vehicle. Water and electric hook-ups, $16 per night; $96 per week. Seniors and handicapped $13 per night; $78 per week per vehicle.

Ten group areas are available by calling (805) 688-4658.No dump station fees.

STORES

Cachuma Store (805) 688-5246 has all types of groceries, firewood, gas station, propane, ice, drinks (including beer and wine), and camping supplies.

Bait, fishing tackle, and licenses can be obtained at Cachuma Boat Rentals. There is a snack bar next to the boat rental and bait shack.

MOTELS

The nearest motels would be in Solvang, 12 miles west.

SPECIAL PROGRAMS

There is a nature center located in back of the general store. This center depicts early California history – local Chumash Indian lore and information on the building of the Bradbury Dam plus information on other local developments. Give it a visit on your next trip to Cachuma. It's really informative.

There are naturalists programs all year round, including a guided two-hour tour of the lake in a large patio boat, slide shows, history, and astronomy.

GENERAL

Lake Cachuma is under the jurisdiction of the Santa Barbara County Parks Department, 610 Mission Canyon, Santa Barbara, CA 93105, Phone (805) 568-2461.

The lake is located in the scenic Santa Ynez Valley which was the home and hunting grounds of the Chumash Indians. Wild life abounds and is protected in the lake area. It is not uncommon to see deer, quail, raccoons, bobcats, and other wild life casually move along the banks where you are fishing from a boat.

Since 1989 the Bald Eagle has returned and established its year round nesting.

Cachuma is a fine fishing lake producing large fish of each species. Some lake records are: large mouth bass, 17 pounds, 9 ounces; small mouth bass, 4 pounds, 14 ounces; cats, 32 pounds, 12 ounces; trout, 14 pounds, 8 ounces; bluegill, 2 pounds, 8 ounces; red ear sunfish, 3 pounds, 4 ounces; crappie, 2 pounds, 8 ounces.

Cachuma Lake is one of the most beautiful lakes in Southern California. Just one trip there and you'll be "hooked"!

GIBRALTAR LAKE

Phone: (805) 564-5387

Elevation 1,400 feet   8,500-Acre Lake

Gibraltar Lake is located approximately 130 miles northwest of Los Angeles. From Los Angeles take Hwy 101 through Santa Barbara to the San Marcos Pass turn-off. Take Hwy 154 over the pass, 18 miles to Paradise Road. Turn right on Paradise Road approximately 12 miles to Redrock Campground. You must park here and walk three miles to the lake.

Gibraltar Lake is open on Fridays, Saturdays, and Sundays during the months of January, February, and March. You must have a valid state fishing license and a $4.00 per day permit. Fishing is permitted from one hour before sunrise until one hour after sunset.

Permits are obtained from the City Recreation Department at 620 Laguna Street, Santa Barbara, CA 93102. Enclose $4.00 for each (2 limit) permit and $1.00 for mailing.

The lake has trout and the limit is 5. Since there is very limited fishing, there should be some whoppers in there. No live bait allowed.

There are restroom facilities at the dam and each fishing area, but no drinking water is provided. Clean fish away from shores.

Refuse containers are furnished, so be sure to can your trash.

There is no body contact, swimming, boating, or fish cleaning in the lake.

Horseback riding – (your horse) is allowed and there is plenty of parking for horse trailers at both Red Rock parking area and Camino Cielo where the access road intersects.

This is a real rough-it type of outing, so go prepared to carry your food and drink in and your fish out.

Gibraltar Lake is under the jurisdiction of the City of Santa Barbara, Department of Public Works, Division of Water Resources, 630 Garden Street, Santa Barbara, CA 93101; Phone: (805) 564-5387.

Marvin B. with a 16.4 Hawg – Cachuma.

JAMESON LAKE
Closed to the Public

o o o o

TWITCHELL LAKE
Closed to the Public

o o o o

ZACA LAKE

Human Potential Foundation
P. O. Box 187, Los Olivos, CA 93441
Phone: (805) 688-4891

Elevation 2,400 feet   Surface Acres 30

Zaca Lake is a private lake. It is located in Los Padres National Forest, 135 miles northwest of Los Angeles. Take Hwy 101 to Santa Barbara, turn right on Hwy 154 over San Marcos Pass, past Lake Cachuma to Los Olivos. Turn right on Foxen Canyon Road and go approximately 12 miles into mountains to lake.

OPEN

Year round from 8 a.m. to sunset for day use.

FEES

$5.00 per adult; $3.00 per child. No license needed.

BOAT RENTALS

Row boats only; $8.00 per hour. Neither gas' nor electric motors allowed. Canoes are available.

BOAT LAUNCH

Car topers only, 14' maximum. No motors allowed. $5.00 fee to launch.

FISH & LIMITS

No fishing.

GENERAL

Cabins only (no cooking facilities) $149.95, summer; $110.00, winter per day for two; $11.00 for extra adult. European plan.

Inside jacuzzi tubs and fireplace.

Two cabins with cooking facilities. Call for rates.

There is a restaurant and lounge open to the public. Also, picnic areas for families and groups.

Overnight camping, add $6.00 to day fee. No dogs allowed.

The facilities are available for business conferences, seminars, and retreats. A place to get away and relax, hike the many trails, swim, bicycle, and play tennis.

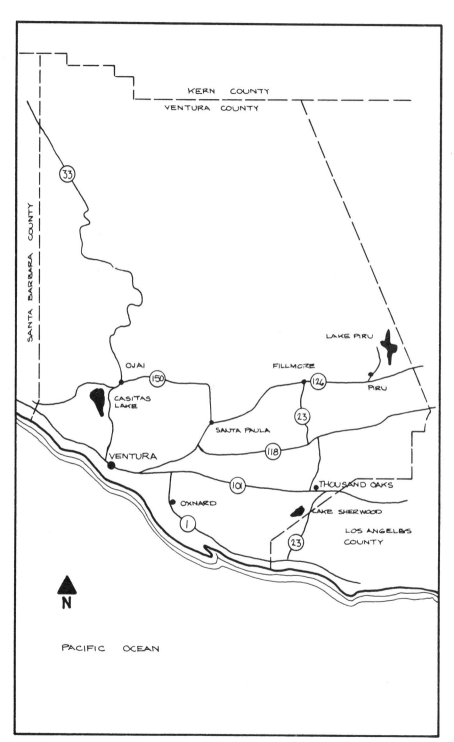

KERN COUNTY

VENTURA COUNTY

SANTA BARBARA COUNTY

(33)

LAKE PIRU

OJAI

(150)

CASITAS LAKE

FILLMORE

(126)

PIRU

SANTA PAULA

(23)

(118)

VENTURA

(101)

THOUSAND OAKS

OXNARD

(1)

LAKE SHERWOOD

(23)

LOS ANGELES COUNTY

N

PACIFIC OCEAN

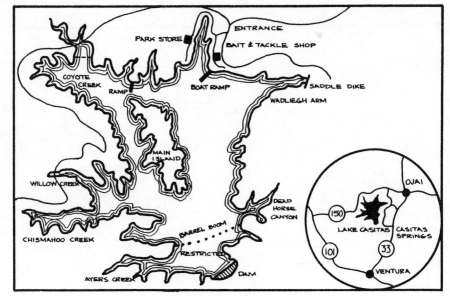

LAKE CASITAS
11311 Santa Ana Road, Ventura, CA 93001
Phone (805) 649-2233

Elevation 600 feet   Surface Acres 2,500

Lake Casitas is located 78 miles from Los Angeles and 12 miles north of Ventura. From Hwy 101 turn north on Hwy 33, continue to Hwy 150, turn left to lake.

OPEN & FEES

Year round, sunrise to sunset for fishing, boating, and picnicking. Twenty-four hours for camping. State fishing license required. No fishing permit is necessary. Motor vehicle permit: $5.00 per day; or $50.00 per year; pets, $1.00 per day. Must be on leash.

BOAT RENTALS

Phone: (805) 649-2043. Your motor, 10 HP maximum.

Rowboats	Weekdays		Weekends & Holidays		Senior Weekdays	
Size	5 Hrs.	Day	5 Hrs.	Day	5 Hrs.	Day
4 Pass.	$15	$19	$19	$24	$12	$15
6 Pass.	$18	$22	$23	$28	$15	$18
With Motor						
4 Pass/6HP	$30	$38	$38	$48	$24	$30
4 Pass/8HP	$42	$52	$51	$64	$34	$42
6 Pass/6HP	$35	$44	$45	$56	$29	$36
6 Pass/8HP	$45	$56	$56	$70	$35	$45

Patio deck boats and paddle boats for rent.

BOAT LAUNCH	There are two excellent paved boat launching ramps. Boat permits are $5.00 per day; or $45.00 per calendar year. Slips – one night, $6.00; one week, $25.00; one month, $50.00. 40 mph speed limit. No canoes or kayaks. Minimum size, 11' with 48" width; maximum size, 24'.
FISH & LIMITS	Bass (12" min. size) – 5; trout – 5; channel cats – 5; crappie – 25; red ear sunfish and green perch – no limit.
FISH CLEANING	Yes. Three excellent facilities, one located on the west side of Santa Ana Creek and one on the main road near "G" Camp, with water, sinks, boards, disposers, and lights for evening cleaning. The third facility is on the north shore.
BAIT	No mudsuckers or minnows other than shad caught in the lake. Crawfish, water dogs, worms, and lures OK.
MOTORBIKES	All operators must have valid operator's license and bikes must be street legal. Riding on roads only. Entrance fees are required for all bikes.
PICNICKING	Yes. There are beautiful oak trees with tables and streams. Plenty of room for hiking and walking.
WATERSKI SWIMMING	No. No waders or tube fishing. No body contact with water allowed.
SAILING	Yes. Conventional design; no catamarans unless hard deck, 12" free board.
CAMPING	Yes. Trailers, campers, and tents; 14-day stay limit. 450 campsites and one overflow site with additional sites. 150 sites have water and electricity, $18.00 per night, summer; $16.00 per night, winter. Other sites with water, modern restrooms, and showers (25¢) are $12.00 and $14.00 per night. Second vehicle is $6.00. Check out time is 2 p.m. Two dump stations available. Reservations may be made in advance with $5.00 reservation fee. Phone (805) 649-1122 – 8 a.m. to 3 p.m. Monday through Friday. Speed limit is 15 mph in park.
STORES	There is a store in the park where you can get bait, licenses, fishing supplies, groceries, firewood, ice, beer, wine, camping and trailer supplies. Snack bar at ramp, open all year. Other stores in Ojai, Oak View & Ventura, from 3 to 12 miles from the lake. Trailer rentals are also available at store: Call (805) 649-1202. Trailer & boat storage, 1-15 days, $19.00; monthly $38.00.
MOTELS	There are numerous motels in nearby Ojai, Oak View and Ventura from 3 to 12 miles from the lake.
GENERAL	Lake Casitas Recreation Area is under the jurisdiction of the Casitas Municipal Water District, P. O. Box 37, Oak View, CA 93022. A new "day use" area on the north shore with additional fish cleaning station, picnic areas, paved road and fishing dock was just completed.

Trout are planted weekly during the winter and largest caught to date was a 9 pounder. Casitas Lake is a good bass and channel cat lake. The record bass was 21 pounds, 3 ounces; while the largest catfish weighted 42 pounds. Red ear sunfish also grow to record size, the largest is 3½ pounds.

A trip to Casitas Lake is a very enjoyable family outing. The large oak trees and rolling hills make it an ideal spot for nature lovers.

Herschell and Scott with 10.2 at Casitas.

John K with 8 and 10 pounders at Casitas

Herschell with Casitas 7.5 pound.

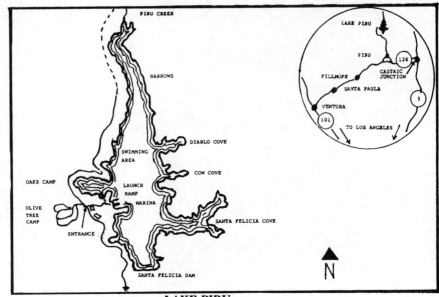

LAKE PIRU

P. O. Box 202, Piru, CA 93040
Phones: Gate (805) 521-1500
Marina (805) 521-1231

Elevation 1,055 feet   Surface Acres 1,200

Lake Piru is located approximately 53 miles northwest of Los Angeles. From Los Angeles take Hwy 5 to the Castaic Junction. Turn left on Hwy 126 and go west approximately 12 miles to the town of Piru. Turn right through Piru, 6 miles to the lake.

OPEN	Sunrise to sunset, year round. Closed Christmas.

FEES
State fishing license required. Vehicle permits:
Auto	$6.00 per day; $60.00 annually
Motorbikes	6.00 per day; 60.00 annually
(Ride on roads only.)	
Bus	50¢ per day per person
Seniors, 65 and up	$55.00 annually
Pets, dogs	$1.00 per day; must be on leash

BOAT RENTALS
Marina (805) 521-1231. No reservations.
Boat only	$23.00 per day; $17.00 half day
With motor	50.00 per day; 25.00 two hours
Slips, $10.00 per night; dry storage, $50.00 per month

BOAT LAUNCH
Five-lane paved ramp, $6.00 per day; $60.00 annually. Minimum size 12', minimum beam 42". 35 mph speed limit.

FISH & LIMITS	Bass (12" min.) – 5; trout – 5; cats – 10; crappie – 25; bluegill and red ear sunfish – no limit. Fish cleaning next to office.
BAIT	No minnows, only shad caught in lake OK. No mudsuckers but waterdogs, crawfish, worms, and lures OK.
BANK FISHING	Yes. No waders. Tube fishing OK in designated areas.
SWIMMING	Yes. Designated areas; summer only: consult office for times and days.
PICNICKING	Yes. New grassy picnic area in Reasoner Canyon with individual and group sites.
WATERSKI	Yes. EXCEPT: All coves, north end of dam area. 5 mph speed limit. No jetskis, water toys OK.
SAILING	Yes. 12' minimum, 42" beam. No surfboards/windsurfers.
MOTORBIKES	Yes. On roads and trails; 8 a.m. to sunset. Must have valid California driver's license, and bike must be registered.
CAMPING	Yes. Campers, trailers, and tents. Reservations can be made by calling (805) 521-1500 Monday through Thursday 8 a.m. to 4 p.m.
	135 spaces, regular. Water faucets and restrooms; free hot showers. $16.00 per night summer, $14.00 winter. 5 spaces – full hook-ups, $22.00 per night.
	106 spaces with electricity, $19.00 per night, 4 people; maximum stay 14 nights in summer; 30 days, winter.
	Pets (dogs) must be on leash. Quiet time: 10 p.m. to 8 a.m. Fires in rings and grills only.
STORES/RESTAURANTS	There is a restaurant and concession at the marina where you can buy meals, sandwiches, drinks, beer, ice, licenses, and supplies.
MOTELS	Fillmore, 14 miles west on Hwy 126 and Hwy 5 to the east.
GENERAL	Lake Piru has proved to be a good fishing lake over the years. Trout are planted by the Department of Fish and Game for year round fishing. Fish grow to exceptionally large size in Piru. The record catches are: Bass, 14 pounds, 7 ounces; catfish, 32 pounds; crappie, 3½ pounds; red ear sunfish weighing 2 pound, 4 ounces.

o o o o

LAKE MATILIJA

Off limits to fishermen.

o o o o

LAKE SHERWOOD

Closed to the Public

o o o o

Scott on the Alamo Run.

Scott with 5½, 5¾ and 6.4 pounds. Clear Lake stock.

Another Casitas 8.5 pounder.

INFLATABLE BOATS

Regulations and Requirements

A Supplement to
"LAKE RECREATION IN SOUTHERN CALIFORNIA FOR WEEKENDERS"

This supplement gives general guidelines covering inflatable boat regulations on lakes in the ten counties in Southern California. In addition to these requirements, your inflatable will be inspected by the local ranger or warden to determine its safety and compliance.

It would be wise for each boat owner to get a copy of the "ABCs OF THE CALIFORNIA BOATING LAW" from the Department of Navigation and Ocean Development in Sacramento. This gives all the State Regulations and Requirements. Page 24 of this pamphlet, entitled "MINIMUM REQUIRED EQUIPMENT", is reproduced by permission of the Department of Navigation and Ocean Development, for your convenience, at the end of this supplement.

The information contained herein was accurate at the time of writing, (September, 1996). The attitude of various lake management groups concerning INFLATABLES has been slowly changing toward permitting the use of the more sturdy types. These changes will be noted in future editions of "LAKE RECREATION IN SOUTHERN CALIFORNIA FOR WEEKENDERS".

This information in your copy of "LAKE RECREATION IN SOUTHERN CALIFORNIA FOR WEEKENDERS" gives you all you will need to plan your lake trip with your inflatable.

IMPERIAL COUNTY

SALTON SEA	No size limit; must be seaworthy; comply with state regulations. One approved life jacket per passenger.
FINNEY-RAMEY	No size limit; seaworthy, no motors.
SUNBEAM WEIST	No size limit; seaworthy and one approved life jacket per passenger.
WISTER UNIT	No boats.
CANALS	No boats allowed.

KERN COUNTY

BUENA VISTA ISABELLA	Minimum 7'11"; must have 2 cells and be powered by wind or motor. If over 1/2 HP, must be minimum of 11'; have state registration, and comply with state regulations.

FRAZIER MING – None.

WOOLLOMES Must be seaworthy; if over 8', must have state CF number.

LOS ANGELES COUNTY

CASTAIC **Big Lake:** 9' minimum; must comply with state regulations.
Lower Lagoon: 8' minimum; seaworthy; electric motors only.

CRYSTAL Minimum 8'; must be seaworthy and have one life vest per person.

ELIZABETH Minimum 8'; state regulations apply; maximum 10 HP motor.

HANSEN DAM Closed for redevelopment

HARBOR (renamed) MACHADO – No private boats.

HUGHES No size limit; must be safe.

JACKSON Small boats only. No motors allowed.

LITTLEROCK No minimum size; seaworthy and conform to state regulations.

MACHADO No private boats.

PUDDING-STONE Minimum 8' without motor; minimum 12' with motor; comply with state and county regulations.

PYRAMID No size limit; must be seaworthy and comply with state regulations. One life vest per person

SANTA FE Minimum 8'; must be seaworthy and conform to state regulations.

COGSWELL No private boats allowed.
EL DORADO
LEGG LAKE
PECK ROAD
QUAIL LAKE
SAN DIMAS RESERVOIR
SAN GABRIEL RESERVOIR

BIG TUJUNGA Closed.
CHATSWORTH
MORRIS DAM
MUNZ

CANALS No boats allowed.

ORANGE COUNTY

ANAHEIM

IRVINE Must be 8' minimum; must be seaworthy; one life vest per
SANTA ANA passenger.
  RIVER LAKES

LAGUNA NIGUEL REGIONAL PARK No private boats.
YORBA REGIONAL PARK

RIVERSIDE COUNTY

CAHUILLA — Three-man minimum size; must be Coast Guard approved. One life saving device per person.

CORONA — Must be 8' min., must be seaworthy, one life vest per person.

ELSINORE
PERRIS — No minimum size; if over 8'; must be state registered; with motor, must have CF # aboard; one approved life jacket per passenger.

REFLECTION — For campers only.

SKINNER — 10' minimum; 3 compartments, floor boards, and state registered.

HEMET — No inflatables, canoes, kayaks, or rubber rafts.

VAIL — Private development

FISHERMAN'S RETREAT - Private development.

ANGLER'S LAKE   No boats allowed.
ELCASCO - FULMOR - PEPPERTREE - RAINBOW

SAN BERNARDINO COUNTY

ARROWHEAD — Only lake property owners may launch boats.

BIG BEAR
JENKS — 12' minimum; Coast Guard approved; comply with state boating regulations. No rafts.

SILVERWOOD — Under 8' restricted area; 8' and above, must be seaworthy and comply with state and county regs.

BALDWIN   No private boats.
CUCAMONGA-GUASTI - GLEN HELEN - GREEN VALLEY - GREGORY - LLOYDS - PELICAN - HORSESHOE - YUCAIPA - MOJAVE NARROWS

SAN DIEGO COUNTY

There are seven lakes in the San Diego City chain for boating. All have the following regulations covering inflatable boats:

EL CAPITAN
HODGES
MIRAMAR
MURRAY
OTAY, LOWER
SAN VICENTE
SUTHERLAND — Minimum 9'x48"x12" deep (centerline), 8" free board loaded. Have bow and stern. Minimum 2 air compartments inflated to specs. Have floor boards. Have min. 50 cu. ft. capacity. No freakish lines. Lake Ranger will determine boat capacity. Must comply with City of San Diego Lakes Rules and Regulations.

CUYAMACA
MORENA — Same as city lakes above.

HENSAW
WOHLFORD — No inflatables, canoes, kayaks, or rubber rafts.

JENNINGS — Yes. Must have hardwood floor and moulded transom.

DIXON	No private boats.
LOVELAND	
POWAY	
SANTEE LAKES	

| BARRETT | No boats allowed. |
| DOAN POND | |

SAN DIEGUITO	Closed to the public.
SWEETWATER	
WINDMILL	

SAN LUIS OBISPO COUNTY

ATASCADERO	No minimum size; must be safe. One life saving device per person.
LOPEZ LAKE	8' minimum, with at least 3 air cells, reinforced bottom; comply with state regulations. No rafts.
NACIMIENTO SAN ANTONIO	Under 8' use restricted area. 8' and over must comply with state boating laws.
SANTA MARGARITA	8' minimum; 3 air cells, reinforced bottom and comply with state boating laws. No rafts.
LAGUNA LAKE	No maximum or minimum size. Must be safe.
OSO FLACO	No minimum. Use at your own risk.
WHALE ROCK RESERVOIR	No boats allowed.

SANTA BARBARA COUNTY

CACHUMA	10' minimum x 42" wide; must have floor boards and comply with state boating laws.
GIBRALTAR	No boats allowed.
ZACA	No minimum size; must be safe; no motors. Maximum 14'.
JAMESON TWITCHELL	Closed.

VENTURA COUNTY

CASITAS	No canoes, kayaks, or rubber rafts. Inflatables must be at least 11' long, 48" wide, with 12" free board. Must have solid floor and transom, multi-air chambers, comply with state laws and display registration and CF numbers.
PIRU	Must be 12'; 3 air compartments, floor boards with at least 3 HP gas engine; must have DMV CF numbers. No canoes, kayaks, or rubber rafts.
MATILIJA SHERWOOD	Closed to the public.

MINIMUM REQUIRED EQUIPMENT

	EQUIPMENT	VESSEL LENGTH			
		(Less than 16 feet)	(16 feet to less than 26 feet)	(26 feet to less than 40 feet)	(40 feet to not more than 65 feet)*
All vessels	PERSONAL FLOTATION DEVICES	One Type I, II, III (wearable) or Type IV (throwable) for each person on board.	A Type I, II, or III (wearable for each person on board and one Type IV (throwable) in each boat.		
	BELL	None.[1]	None.[1]	One, which when struck, produces a clear, bell-like tone of full round characteristics.	
	WHISTLE	None.[1]	One hand, mouth, or power operated audible at least ½ mile.	One hand or power operated, audible at least 1 mile.	One power operated, audible at least 1 mile.
All motorboats	FIRE EXTINGUISHER—PORTABLE When NO fixed fire extinguishing system is installed in machinery space(s).	At least One B-I type approved hand portable fire extinguisher.[3]		At least Two B-I type approved hand portable fire extinguishers; OR at least One B-II type approved hand portable fire extinguisher.	At least Three B-I type approved hand portable fire extinguishers; OR at least One B-I type Plus One B-II type approved hand portable fire extinguisher.
	When fixed fire extinguishing system is installed in machinery space(s).	None.	None.	At least One B-I type approved hand portable fire extinguisher.	At least Two B-I type approved hand portable fire extinguishers; OR at least One B-II type approved hand portable fire extinguisher.
		B-I Type Approved Hand Portable Fire Extinguishers contain: Foam, 1¼ up to 2½ gallons; Freon, 2½ pounds; or Carbon Dioxide, 4 up to 15 pounds; or Dry Chemical, 2 up to 10 pounds.[2] B-II Type Approved Hand Portable Fire Extinguishers contain: Foam, 2½ gallons, or Carbon Dioxide, 15 pounds; or Dry Chemical, 10 up to 20 pounds.			
	BACK-FIRE FLAME CONTROL	One approved device on each carburetor of all gasoline engines installed after April 25, 1940, except outboard motors.			
	VENTILATION	At least two ventilator ducts fitted with cowls or their equivalent for the purpose of properly and efficiently ventilating the bilges of every engine and fuel-tank compartment of boats using gasoline or other fuel of a flashpoint less than 110° F.			

[1] NOTE.—Not required specifically by the law, but these vessels are required to sound proper signals under certain conditions.

[2] NOTE.—Toxic vaporizing-liquid type fire extinguishers, such as those containing carbon tetrachloride or chlorobromomethane, are not acceptable as required extinguishers.

[3] NOTE.—Exceptions: A motorboat of any of the following types is not required to carry a fire extinguisher:
(A) Less than 26 feet in length of an open construction, propelled by an outboard motor, and not carrying passengers for hire.

1. A vessel of "open construction" is one which does not have enclosed areas in which inflammable vapors may collect. A vessel is of "open construction" if it has, during all conditions of operations, adequate natural ventilation of all areas subject to penetration by inflammable vapors.
(B) Propelled by electric motors of 10 horsepower or less.
(C) Engaged in any race which has been previously arranged or announced or while engaged in such navigation as is incidental to the tuning up of the motorboat and engines for the race.

* For specific requirements for vessels over 65', consult legal text.

For Complete Information, see current edition of ABCs of the California Boating Law.

ORDER BLANK

MAIL TO: Herschell Whitmer Associates
             P. O. Box 7261
             Long Beach, CA 90807

Please send me _____ copies of *Lake Recreation in Southern California for Weekenders*. I am enclosing my check for $12.94 ($11.95 + 99¢) for each copy.

MY NAME IS _____

MY ADDRESS IS _____

CITY _____ ZIP _____

PLEASE INCLUDE YOUR ZIP CODE

ORDER BLANK

MAIL TO: Herschell Whitmer Associates
             P. O. Box 7261
             Long Beach, CA 90807

Please send me _____ copies of *Lake Recreation in Southern California for Weekenders*. I am enclosing my check for $12.94 ($11.95 + 99¢) for each copy.

MY NAME IS _____

MY ADDRESS IS _____

CITY _____ ZIP _____

PLEASE INCLUDE YOUR ZIP CODE

ORDER BLANK

MAIL TO: Herschell Whitmer Associates
             P. O. Box 7261
             Long Beach, CA 90807

Please send me _____ copies of *Lake Recreation in Southern California for Weekenders*. I am enclosing my check for $12.94 ($11.95 + 99¢) for each copy.

MY NAME IS _____

MY ADDRESS IS _____

CITY _____ ZIP _____

PLEASE INCLUDE YOUR ZIP CODE
